DID NOAH INVENT TENNIS?

AN HISTORIC MISCELLANY

FASCINATING FACTS AND
EVERYDAY PHRASES EXPLAINED

Peter Ryding

PATHFINDER

Published by Pathfinder Partners Ltd.

ISBN 0-9551525-1-8
ISBN 978-0-9551525-1-1

Designed by Oxford Designers & Illustrators

Cover design by Baseline Arts Ltd., Oxford

Illustrated by Chris Rothero

Produced By Paperhat

For
Louise, Edward, Richard and Monty

Acknowledgements

I would like to take this opportunity to thank everyone who has so enthusiastically embraced and supported the WINKT project from its inception: The many dinner guests who have patiently listened, challenged and in some cases politely fallen asleep whilst I have shared my latest linguistic discoveries; Steve, the guy in the pub who challenged me to write the first book; Peter at ODI, who has been a stalwart supporter and always kept a sense of humour despite everything (and there have been lots of 'things'!); Chris, my artist, who has kept going through the crazy requests that I have made of him; Gillian, who has challenged and checked and added her own ideas despite an apparently endless set of iterations.

Of the many others, who are too many to fit on one page but who have encouraged me throughout, I would like to thank Crisspy the Duck and his friends, Simon, Neil, Spence, Tim (Nadia), Sam (Jo), Hutch, Gordon, Alexander The Great and Henry V, all of whom have played their roles, plus the designer of the keel of the boat, without whom we would all have drowned.

Also thanks to the many members of WINKT the club who continue to write in with both intriguing questions and fascinating discoveries.

Thanks to every one of you.

Contents

Preface

Imagine you are a foreigner who has just learnt the basics of the English language. You proudly walk into a room of native English speakers and listen to their conversation.

'Was it a cock-up you ask? I should bally say so! But it's a good job he had an extra string to his bow because they had him running from pillar to post in that job. His boss's ideas were so off the wall that it wound him up something proper. No wonder he's legged it!'

You may well think you had been on the wrong course!

But it's not just the phrases we use that make English tough to learn and a joy to use. Our language has absorbed more subtleties and richness from other nations than any other. Indeed, English is by far the most widely used official language in the world. We also have the largest vocabulary in the world, at over 250,000 words in the *Oxford English Dictionary*. Having said that, we each tend to pick from our own favourite 2–3,000 most of the time, rarely stepping outside our comfort zone. To put this into context, Shakespeare used over 21,000 words and a top scrabble player will know over 80,000 words!

So, with all this richness and precision at our fingertips, such that we can intuitively distinguish between a simple 'room' and a grander 'chamber' (in a way that many languages cannot), what do we do? We dredge up obscure phrases that often arose for reasons that are no longer relevant and that people don't really understand anyway. Or, even worse, ones that they misunderstand. For example, imagine the foreigner who overhears that something is 'cheap at half the price'. What does that mean? Is it saying that it would be cheap if it was half the current price? In other words, that it is expensive? Or is it saying that it is cheap because it is half the price you were expecting to pay? If *we* are not sure – what chance do foreigners have?

In many cases phrases have simply gone wrong over the ages. For example, take 'the exception that proves the rule.' Pardon? Are we saying that finding an exception to a rule somehow proves that the rule is correct? Surely that has to be utter tosh!

It is only through patient research and an understanding of our heritage that we can make sense of such expressions. In this case the explanation goes back to the Normans' invasion of England in 1066 and their desire to have a clear set of rules with which they could govern the country. The trouble was that the barely literate Anglo-Saxons had few written laws. Most were simply 'known' to those who dispensed justice. However, the Normans passed a law that said that if someone could prove beyond doubt that there was an exception to a law, then by implication that would prove, in another case, that the law did exist. For example, a trader who had a pass allowing him to travel at night after the curfew hour – literally, the hour at which the fire (*feu*) had to be covered (*couvert*) – would prove that the law of curfew did exist. This in turn would enable the

prosecution of someone who broke the curfew. Hence, an exception to a rule does not in fact prove that the rule is correct. However it does proves that the rule exists!

Yet another example of things going wrong is the phrase 'Don't spoil the ship for a hap'orth of tar!' Now, tar may be cheap, but a hap'orth (that's half a penny's worth for those born after 1980) of it does not go far when you are trying to waterproof an entire ship! In fact, by digging into the past we discover that the saying originally referred not to a ship at all but rather to a humble *sheep*! The reason is that just about the only help you could give a sheep with an open sore or wound was to slap on a dollop of tar. This would at

least close the wound and was of course worth doing – especially given the financial value of sheep in medieval days, when they produced the vast majority of England's income. After all, without them we could not have afforded to fight the French through the Hundred Years War! And let's face it, you don't often get the chance to humiliate the entire French nation like we did at the battles of Crécy, Poitiers and Agincourt! Well worth a hap'orth of tar so that we don't spoil the *sheep*!

However, the story is not all mistakes and misunderstandings. Some derivations are a sheer joy to discover. Like the Greek god who used to jump out on humans and scare them away

from his personal harem of nymphs and dryads. His name was Pan, from which we get the word PANIC! Or the need for sailors to be flogged up on the main deck because down below in the cramped conditions there was NOT ENOUGH ROOM TO SWING A CAT – o' nine tails! Why nine tails? Because the Royal Navy decided that the normal three-headed scourge representing the Father, the Son and the Holy Ghost was not 'holy enough' for wicked sailors and so created a 'trinity of holy trinities'. Hence nine tails that left deep scratches on the skin just like the claws of a CAT. And of course the scars would then stay with the troublemaker for the rest of his life, making him a MARKED MAN!

There is also the wonderful realization that so often when different words sound similar they are in fact the same word,

or at least come from the same original source. For example, cheque books, checkmate in chess, checklists, rain checks, the checks (bills) you get in American restaurants, the game of chequers, checkered patterns, the Chancellor of the Exchequer, Chequers pub signs, the prime minister's country house Chequers and simply 'checking something out', all derive from medieval military coups in Persia! Wonderful!

Having studied our language hand in hand with our history for over two decades, I am still surprised, amazed and delighted at what treasures I uncover on a regular basis. Creating this series of books has been a massive and painstaking undertaking, bringing a lot of pleasure and at times a lot of frustration. I just hope that you have fun with the books and that you will find something fascinating, insightful and intriguing within each book that makes you say 'Well, I Never Knew That!' And of course, when you do, please tell your friends and join WINKT the club at www.winkt.com – and vote for WINKT to became a new word in the English language! Thank you for doing so.

Don't just enjoy the English language – CREATE IT!

How to use this book

This book has been written in a unique format so that you can enjoy it in several different ways:

1. You can **read it cover to cover** as an adventure into the rich stories and interconnectedness behind our language.

2. You can **flick to a page** and discover fascinating facts bit by bit.

3. You can **study the pictures** at the start of each chapter and try to work out the sayings that await you inside.

4. You can **seek out specific words** and sayings via the index.

5. You can **use it as a quiz book** on your own or spoken out loud with friends, by reading each paragraph and then stopping just before the CAPITALS reveal the answers.

6. You can just leave it in the loo for everyone to enjoy. But beware – your guests may not come out for some time! And, of course, when they do they are bound to say – 'Well, I Never Knew That!'

1

From Real Tennis
to Lawn Tennis

Did you know that we owe the pleasures of
Wimbledon to medieval Moors and monks?
Read on . . .

Well, I never knew that . . .
. . . tennis is scored 'love all, 15, 30, 40, game'
because of eggs, clocks and Noah's Ark!

T he medieval Arabs used to play a game in which they hit a ball to each other with their hands. It was initially spread to Spain by the invading Moors and then taken up by Christian knights and churchmen during the crusades of the 11th and 12th centuries. They in turn took it back with them to their homelands, where it became especially popular in the French monasteries. Before one player served, he would shout 'Take this!' – or, in French, 'Tenez!' Over time the word, and the activity, evolved into an early form of what in England we call TENNIS.

In the monasteries the game was played in the courtyards, hence the phrase TENNIS COURT.

Henry VIII played a great deal of this game at his purpose-built tennis courtyard in HAMPTON COURT.

The Latin word *regalis* (meaning royal) evolved into a shorter word both in Spain, where it is still used today, and in England, where it is used only in conjunction with this form of tennis, giving us REAL TENNIS. Incidentally, in Spain the word is used, for example, to describe the 'royal' city of Madrid where the King lived: REAL MADRID.

The monastic courtyards would usually have sloping roofs over the surrounding passageways or cloisters, held up by pillars. This is still used as the basic design of real tennis courts. Initially a piece of rope was strung across the courtyard to divide it into two parts, with each player needing to play into his opponent's area. Hence the phrase THE BALL IS IN YOUR COURT – nowadays meaning 'it is now your turn or responsibility'.

To make it easier to see who won the point, the rope evolved into a net. Where necessary, posts would be sunk into the ground from which the net was hung. One strategy in the game can be to play close to the net with one shot and then to the back of the court near the pillars of the old cloisters, and so on, to wear your opponent out. Hence the phrase FROM PILLAR TO POST, meaning running all over the place.

In real tennis it is important to make the ball bounce as close to certain lines as possible. This creates an advantage called a 'chase' that can, in fact, suddenly win a game. This can best be achieved by hitting the ball with the racquet at a sharp (cutting) angle, a tactic which gives us the phrase to CUT TO THE CHASE – to come to the point immediately.

Monks would make balls out of cloth tied with string and initially used their hands to hit the ball. Hence the different terms for hitting a ball: BACKHAND AND FOREHAND. In France a version of the game is still called *jeu de paume* – the game of the palm.

To avoid hurting their hands, players often copied the Arabic tradition of wrapping a length of cloth called *ruqatwas* around their hand. This gives us the word RACQUET. Incidentally, the racquet used in real tennis is unique in that it is non-symmetrical and still made from wood rather than carbon fibre. It is shaped like a giant palm with one side flat, representing the part next to the little finger, and one side rounded, like the side where the thumb is.

Scoring was done using the quarter-hours on the monastery clock, which is how we have ended up with 15, 30, 45 AND GAME. The third number, however, was close to another

number that had strong biblical connections and so it was changed to that number: 40. It rained on the ark for 40 days and 40 nights; Moses went to Mount Sinai for 40 days; Jesus was in the wilderness for 40 days; and so on. The shape of an egg gives rise to the word describing a nil score: LOVE, from *l'oeuf*, French for 'the egg', and the shape of zero. The shape of an egg has also given rise to different phrases for a score of zero in ball games: in the UK a DUCK, in the US a GOOSE. Also, when someone tries something that does not work it can be said that they have just LAID AN EGG, meaning they have produced zero benefit.

When two tennis players tied at a score of 40, it was agreed that instead of just one more point to win, either player would need two clear points to win. Thus we get the word DEUCE – from *deux*, French for two.

Given the nature of the original cloisters, with gaps between the pillars, a rule developed that is still key to real tennis that the ball must always be served so that it makes contact with a roof first and then drops down into the court. Because different monasteries had different shaped courtyards there was no standard court. However, the game always involved hitting balls onto various roofs and walls, and part of the skill was trying to anticipate the unpredictable angles at which the ball would rebound off them. This gives us the phrase OFF THE WALL, meaning an unusual angle, or new idea.

In tennis, and some other sports, players can be ranked by their likelihood of winning, so that matches can be arranged to avoid leading players meeting one another in the early rounds of a competition, so saving the closest-fought matches for the later rounds. Using an analogy with the gardener's practice of carefully spacing plants to avoid unnecessary competition for good soil, or premature weeding out of potentially good plants, we get the phrase SEEDING of competitors.

A variety of tennis played in France, called *bande*, ended up having more emphasis upon hitting the ball with the wooden part of the racquet. A similar game in Ireland, with some similarities to lacrosse, involved hitting a wooden object around between players on a flat piece of ground, sometimes played on ice. This game was also called *bande*. From this idea of hitting the ball around among several players we get the phrase BANDIED ABOUT. The stick used was a distinctive shape, having a long straight handle with a flat end bent at a sharp angle. This gave us the phrase for people with bent or bow legs: BANDY-LEGGED. And this game eventually evolved into what we know as hockey.

Incidentally for centuries tennis courts resembling monastic courtyards were built across England. However the sheer cost of doing so eventually led to a new version of the game that could be played in the open without major construction costs. This is what we know as LAWN TENNIS !

2

From Brawling to Boxing

Life has a way of handing out some hard knocks,
so perhaps it's not surprising that fighting sports
have given us a lot of phrases we use without
ever going near a boxing ring!

Well, I never knew that . . .
. . . if you get shirty you might not be laughing when the
punchline comes

In the 19th century, when gentlemen disagreed about something and wished to fight, it was considered unseemly to fight while dressed – that would be too much like common men brawling. So they would at least undress to their shirts, and often remove these as well. Hence the phrase meaning that someone is getting ready for a fight: GETTING SHIRTY. If, however, you preferred to calm things down and avoid a physical confrontation you would say: 'KEEP YOUR SHIRT ON.'

In both boxing and horse racing, contestants have to be weighed before an event and the weight, which is then publicly announced, can significantly affect how people bet on them. It is also a point of no return, after which contestants are wholly committed to going through with the event to the final outcome. From this we get the phrase meaning that someone is committing themselves wholeheartedly to a situation: WEIGHING IN.

In boxing, consistent blows to the body can wear an opponent down, and if the hitter is lucky, such a punch may catch his opponent unguarded and wind him, significantly reducing his ability to fight back. Hence we call any serious impact a BODY BLOW.

To move around the ring boldly poking your chin out as if you are happy for it to be hit and challenging the opponent to try is an act of extreme confidence: TO LEAD WITH THE CHIN. Sometimes a tough boxer does take a hit but doesn't go down. He carries on fighting as if untroubled by the blow, even though it must have hurt him. Hence the phrase we use for someone who suffers criticism, a setback or a firm rebuke, but accepts it and carries on anyway: TAKING IT ON THE CHIN.

When a person is convulsed with laughter, after hearing the end of a good joke, he often grabs his belly, as if he had been hit in the gut: so we call the climax of the joke the PUNCHLINE.

Well, I never knew that . . .
. . . losing your bottle means you won't
come up to scratch

In the days of bare-knuckle boxing there were very few rules. One of them was that two lines would be scratched in the mud a few feet apart, and then each boxer would put the tip of one foot up against the line before commencing the

fight, so that he was TOEING THE LINE. If one boxer was knocked down or if the referee had to restart the fight, both boxers had to put their foot on the line again within 30 seconds or lose the match; if one of them didn't, then he hadn't COME UP TO [THE] SCRATCH. Also, from the referee's instruction for boxers to get ready, 'get set to the scratch', we have a phrase that simply means a fight:

a SET TO. Later, a time limit of ten seconds was set for a boxer to get back on his feet or lose the fight; if he didn't get up then, he was OUT FOR THE COUNT. If a boxer is knocked down, possibly rendered unconscious, and counted out before he can regain his feet, he has clearly lost the fight and is DOWN AND OUT. Another meaning of the same phrase is that someone has fallen upon very hard times and is probably living below their previous station in life: 'down in life and out of luck'.

When we want to say that something fits the bill completely, we use the phrase created to describe a fighter who comes to the mark in the ground confidently, when told to do so by the referee, looking fit and ready for the fight: he was said to have

COME UP TO THE MARK. Likewise, when we think that someone's behaviour is beyond the limits of acceptability, we describe it in the same way as a boxer who is so keen to start the fight that he steps forward past the mark in the ground before the referee has signalled the start of the round: he is said to have OVERSTEPPED THE MARK.

A lot of money could be bet on boxing matches, and so if a decision was marginal there would often be a great deal of argument and shouting to try to get the judges to change their minds. Of course, this did not happen as everyone knew that the decisions were final and not open to discussion. Nevertheless, the arguments would carry on, giving us the expression ALL OVER BAR THE SHOUTING.

Boxing is a very strenuous activity, leading to dehydration, so boxers need a lot of water, and the bottle of water was an important part of a boxer's support. If a boxer was getting injured and losing a fight, his seconds would sometime use a phrase meaning that he could not carry on: he had LOST HIS BOTTLE. We use the same phrase today to mean that someone has lost his nerve.

If a boxer was clearly taking a beating and the bell sounded to end the round, allowing him a short time in which to recover, it was said that he had been SAVED BY THE BELL. However, once it became clear that he was going to lose the fight, his seconds could accept defeat by tossing a towel into the centre of the ring – THROWING IN THE TOWEL. And

sometimes a boxer who had had enough would say 'COUNT ME OUT' – as we do nowadays when we want to withdraw from something.

At fairgrounds, bare-knuckle boxers would issues challenges to all-comers, with cash prizes for the winner. Those who accepted the challenge would pitch their hats into the fighting arena. From this we get the phrase THROWING YOUR HAT INTO THE RING.

To avoid serious injuries, gloves were gradually introduced and eventually bare-knuckle boxing was outlawed. However, occasionally two fighters who hated each other would

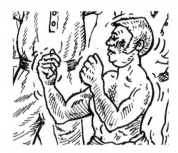

sometimes revert to the more dangerous form of fighting. Hence the phrase THE GLOVES ARE OFF, or TO TAKE ONE'S GLOVES OFF – meaning making a confrontation more aggressive and doing everything possible to harm the other side.

In boxing, if you are losing, tired and battered, there is a tendency to avoid fighting and to back away around the ring; but, as the saying goes, YOU CAN RUN BUT YOU CAN'T HIDE. Sometimes a tired boxer would fall back onto the ropes around the edge of the ring, from where we get the phrase ON THE ROPES to refer to someone who is really up against it.

Over two thousand years ago Herodotus, one of the greatest commentators of the ancient world, said: 'The thunderbolts of the gods chastise the more enormous animals!' At the start of the 20th century Bob Fitzsimmons, a small boxer who was famous for beating bigger opponents, was asked if he was intimidated by larger boxers. He famously replied: 'THE BIGGER THEY ARE, THE HARDER THEY FALL' – which became his catchphrase.

Well, I never knew that . . .
. . . if you fight by London Rules you don't pull your punches

From the wooden blocks shaped like heads on which wigs used to be displayed we get the term for a head: BLOCK. For example, someone who is as unintelligent as a piece of wood is called a BLOCKHEAD. And someone warning a boxer against sticking his chin out would say: 'IF YOU STICK YOUR NECK OUT YOU WILL GET YOUR BLOCK KNOCKED OFF.' This has given rise to shorter sayings: "DON'T STICK YOUR NECK OUT" and "I'LL KNOCK YOUR BLOCK OFF".

Bare-knuckle fights would always result in bleeding injuries to the face and to the boxers' own hands, as bone crunched into bone. The skin and flesh round the knuckles would often

be particularly badly torn, with the bones almost showing through. Hence the phrase NEAR THE KNUCKLE.

A full power punch is delivered with the boxer's full bodyweight behind it. An alternative is to pull back at the last moment to either land a much lighter punch or not make any contact at all: TO PULL ONE'S PUNCHES.

In boxing, blows can come up from below – an UPPER CUT – or be delivered directly with a horizontal blow, like a direct and honest statement: STRAIGHT FROM THE SHOULDER.

When a person has completed what he or she set out to do, despite the difficulties encountered along the way, they are described in the same way as a boxer who sees a fight through to the end of the final round: he is said to have GONE THE DISTANCE.

Boxers are classified into categories of weights to ensure approximately fair and safe contests. One very light weight category in boxing is named after a very aggressive and plucky but small breed of chicken found in south-east Asia: BANTAM weight. If a boxer successfully takes on an opponent from a higher weight category he is said to be PUNCHING ABOVE HIS WEIGHT.

Around 1840 new rules were introduced to focus fights on boxing instead of gouging, kicking or head-butting. However,

the audiences in London preferred to see the blood and dirty tricks, and so the rules were usually ignored there. Hence a term came to mean that no rules would be applied: LONDON RULES.

In 1867 a new set of the standard rules of boxing were drawn up to govern the sport in Britain. They were endorsed and named after John Sholto Douglas, better known by his aristocratic title, the Marquess of Queensberry. Hence the new regulations were called the QUEENSBERRY RULES. Among other things, they prohibited punches aimed anywhere near the groin. Hence the phrase for any action or comment that hurts someone else (physically or not) but is considered cheating: BELOW THE BELT.

3

Bankers and Business

Trade and commerce have always been at the heart
of British life – so it's not surprising that they are
well entrenched in our language as well.

LOMB

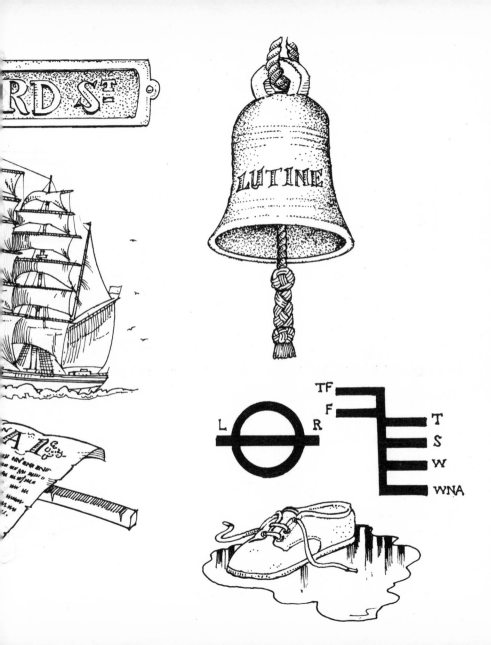

Well, I never knew that . . .
. . . the rancher who branded his cattle with
no mark at all is now world-famous

This term originally came from an old word meaning 'to burn'. It was initially used to describe a torch with a burning flame on the end so that people could see in the dark: a BRAND. It was then used to describe irons in a fire that were so hot that they gave off a red or even white heat so that a blacksmith could hammer them into shape. When such an iron object was finished it would still be hot and giving off light, and was therefore called BRAND NEW. Some pieces of metal were designed to mark livestock by burning their coats with the hot iron, called a BRANDING IRON. This idea of marking something to make it stand out as different from others' livestock was then adopted by business as a PRODUCT BRAND.

In the 19th century a Texan cattle rancher refused to brand his cattle. He then claimed that any cattle he came across that were not branded were his! Hence, strays and other cattle that walked away from any herd began to be called by the rancher's name. The name has stuck and is now widely used to describe people who do not conform and have a tendency to separate themselves from the herd. The rancher's name was Samuel MAVERICK!

Well, I never knew that . . .
. . . one of the world's most famous brands is the
shape of a keystone

In 1892 the founder of an American food company who very much liked the numbers 7 and 5 created a new advertising campaign and packaging theme based around the number of products that they were then manufacturing: 57 VARIETIES. His name was Henry John HEINZ. He was very proud of his country and his state of Pennsylvania, and as it was nicknamed the 'Keystone State', because it was at the heart of the first 13 states in America, he insisted that the company logo should always be a particular shape – that of a KEYSTONE. It has remained so to this day.

An aero-engine company created in Bavaria later expanded into motor-car manufacture, initially by making British cars under licence. Its logo is an art deco symbolic representation of a rotating propeller. That company is the Bayerische Motoren Werke: BMW. The blue quadrants represent the blue sky and the white quadrants represent a spinning propeller.

A recent perfume brand was named after the left bank of the Seine in Paris, where the exciting and romantic 'Latin quarter' is situated: *RIVE GAUCHE* – literally 'left bank'.

Well, I never knew that . . .
. . . some sheets of paper are named after a court jester

In 1455 Johannes Gutenberg made the first printed book. His business was named after the device he used for printing (in which the paper and type were literally pressed together) and nowadays is used to describe the world of journalists and their publications: THE PRESS. His business was called the Gutenberg Press. An Englishman living in Holland came across Gutenberg's business and took the idea back to England, where he set up the first printing business here. That English-man was William Caxton, founder of THE CAXTON PRESS.

Initially presses were individually designed with no standard sizes. Over time, cost economies drove the industry towards standardized presses and standardized sizes of paper. The manufacturer and the size of the paper would often be indicated by a watermark. This was impressed into the paper while it was still wet and became associated with the size of paper that each manufacturer used. One of the earliest watermarks used on paper was the distinctive court jester's hat and bells or 'fool's cap' – giving us the word FOOLSCAP.

The Romans wrote all letters as capital letters in a very upright style. This was partly, at least, to facilitate carving. Carving the line was relatively easy, but ending a line neatly was difficult. A custom developed whereby the end of each line was flattened off and extended slightly to the left and right to enable the chisel to provide a clean and neat end to the line. This feature is called a serif, and the font is called ROMAN or nowadays, after the famous London newspaper which adopted it, TIMES ROMAN. Incidentally, the reason why all Roman inscriptions are written in block capitals is that they never invented small letters! It was only centuries later that the idea arose of making writing easier by using flowing script and joined-up letters. Shortly after they appeared, a particularly stylish version originated from Venice in Italy and so became known as *Italica* or, as we now call it, ITALIC. Initially the small letter 'I' was just a smaller version of the block capital. But two letter 'I's (without dots) adjacent to each other, for example in the word radii, look very similar to the letter 'u'. Hence it was decided to differentiate the small version of the letter by adding a dot above every 'I', making 'i'. At the time the symbol 'i' was interchangeable for what we now consider to be a different letter and so this too adopted the dot: 'j'. It was only in the 19th century that the different uses and sounds of 'i' and 'j' were formalized.

In printing, 'tittles' (sometimes shortened to 't') are small marks associated with letters – for example, the dot on the stalk of an 'i' is a tittle. Getting these details correct was considered very important and resulted in the phrase 'done to a tittle' or, as we say, DONE TO A T, meaning done perfectly. This association then led to another phrase describing the need for attention to detail: DOTTING THE 'I'S AND CROSSING THE 'T'S.

Well, I never knew that . . .
. . . Westminster burnt down when the government stopped tallying up! No wonder MPs are a laughing stock

The word 'stock' used to mean a tree trunk or other very large or important wooden post, as opposed to a much smaller 'stick'. From this we get many words and phrases. The place of punishment on a village green built around one or two large posts was the STOCKS. If you had committed an offence you would be locked in position and people could throw rotten eggs at you, so you would get EGG ON YOUR FACE, and consequently be laughed at, a LAUGHING STOCK. Stocks, incidentally, were not made illegal until well into the 19th century. Then we have the phrase meaning standing stationary like a tree: STANDING STOCK STILL. A partially built ship would lean up against large posts to keep it upright. This gives us a phrase that nowadays applies to any form of goods

not yet finished or sold: ON THE STOCKS. From there we get the generic word for goods that are in hand and not yet sold, STOCK.

Once a reserve of stock was built up, it would need it to be stacked. Such a stack has given us the word meaning a reserve, a STOCKPILE. Reviewing the pile of stock to check what is there is a STOCK CHECK, and when we want to review any situation we say we will TAKE STOCK. Given the similarity of straight human legs to tree trunks, they too were sometimes called 'stocks', giving us the name of leg coverings, STOCKINGS. The part of a rifle or musket that is designed to to be held firmly against the shoulder when firing, made of wood and designed to make sure that the gun does not move around when the trigger is pulled, is called a STOCK. The old firing mechanisms involved a rotating piece of metal that lowered a smouldering match into a pan of gunpowder. As this movement was reminiscent of a key turning in a lock, the mechanism was called a 'lock'. Hence the expression that originally described the three parts of a gun and is now used to describe the entirety of something: LOCK, STOCK AND BARREL.

The use of the word 'stock' to describe goods that were very similar led to the use of the word meaning a standard item: STOCK ITEM. This, in turn, led to a type of motor racing where the chassis are standard although the body-shells can be very different: STOCK CAR RACING.

Then we have the central line of a family tree: THE FAMILY STOCK. Also, a suitable wife or husband for one's own child would be OF GOOD STOCK. Incidentally, an area of London is named after a well that was by a large tree-stump: STOCKWELL.

Very closely related to the word 'stock' is the word for a cutting from a tree, a STICK. Medieval kings would often need loans from rich nobles to finance building work or foreign wars. When the king needed to borrow money the details would be recorded on specially made hazel-sticks. These sticks were typically a foot long, an inch deep and two inches wide. Grooves or notches would be accurately cut into them to represent the amount of the loan, the interest, and the date of repayment. The stick would then be split down the middle (easy to do with hazel wood) and one half kept by each party. From the French word *tailler*, meaning 'to cut', these pieces of wood became known as TALLY STICKS. When repayment was due the lender's half of the stick would be presented and matched against the government tally stick. This matching of the two pieces was called TALLYING. The calculation of the amount owed, and then paying it, was called TALLYING UP. The person who kept the king's tallies and looked after the payments and receipts for these amounts was known as a TELLER (from *taillier*), from which we get the job title in banks: BANK TELLER.

Such tally sticks were also used by merchants who borrowed money to fund expeditions abroad and would promise a share of the profits instead of interest. Here the lender would keep his half of the tally stick and then hand it in to claim his part of the profits when the ships returned. Clearly, the value of the tally stick was far higher than the worth of the wood itself, and so they were named after a whole tree instead of just a small stick. Hence we get the word still used today to describe part ownership in companies and business ventures: STOCK. The other half of the hazel stick was called 'counterstock'. As these pieces of wood had a real value they could be bought and sold, and this was known as the STOCK MARKET. As this became more organized, a building arose in each major town that became known as the STOCK EXCHANGE. As trade became more sophisticated, such deals had to be spelt out in more detail, and soon it was necessary to use paper to explain the FINE PRINT associated with each 'stock'. Before long, the pieces of wood were more of a hindrance than help, and so they were dropped and replaced by pieces of paper. As these described what proportion or share of the profits each person was entitled to take, they became known as SHARES. These too could be bought and sold, and whoever had possession of the piece of paper when profits were distributed took that share of the profits. Hence the phrase SHAREHOLDER. Incidentally, as lending money to the government was always considered a more robust and safer option than lending to commercial venturers, and as the government kept using the old tally stick systems long after merchants had changed to using paper, we still use the phrase GOVERNMENT STOCK, whereas we tend to call commercial ownership SHARES. Interestingly, America had gained its independence from Britain by the time these changes were taking place, and to this day the word 'stock' is used much more widely in the USA for both government and private ownership.

The old Norse word *skor*, meaning a 'notch', gives us the word for a deep mark or scratch: SCORE. Shepherds and other herdsmen taking their animals to market would record the number of animals on a wooden tally stick. Each animal would be recorded by a notch, with the twentieth being a deeper mark for easy reckoning later. Hence we get the term representing the number 20: A SCORE.

In medieval days paper and pens were rare, so wooden sticks were used as tallies for keeping scores in games, each point being recorded with a small nick cut with a knife. If an important goal or point was scored towards the end of the competition it was called a 'nick in time', or as we know it IN THE NICK OF TIME.

Incredible as it sounds, tally sticks were still being used by the government into the 19th century. When they were replaced with paper, the massive pile of sticks was burnt for heating in the Houses of Parliament. These sticks were the perfect fuel, fully dried out and ideal kindling-shaped pieces for the furnace. Unfortunately in 1834 the furnace was overfilled and when the men went outside for a break the fire quickly got out of control and burnt the Houses of Parliament down. The Gothic-style architecture we see today dates from the rebuilding after this disaster.

Because of the relatively sharp nature of a stick versus a log-like 'stock', the word became associated with piercing. Hence to stab someone is to STICK THEM. This is clearly an unpleasant way to die, and so we have the phrase COME TO A STICKY END. A pig pierced end to end by a spit to be cooked over a fire is a 'STUCK' PIG – that is, a pig that has been 'sticked'. The sense of a stick being firmly pushed into the ground so that it is difficult to remove gives us the word meaning just that: STUCK. If you stick something in the ground so that it is protruding and clearly visible for all to see it is said to STICK UP. A person who is always making themselves noticeable with the intention of arousing admiration is STUCK UP. A robber holding someone at gunpoint may well tell their victim to put their arms straight up: 'STICK 'EM UP!' In the Roman Senate, anyone who wanted to speak always had to stand up first. Hence defending the reputation of someone else meant that you would literally STAND UP FOR THEM. This motion of becoming visible by standing upright can also be described as STICKING UP FOR THEM.

Another image derived from the use of a 'stick' to pierce something led to a new meaning. For example, a brooch would be 'stuck on' using the pin. This led to the word being used to describe the use of a pin to 'stick' two pieces of paper together. When the use of adhesives became more popular, the phrase was transferred to this new way of STICKING things together. This in turn led to any 'tacky' substance being described as STICKY. Hence in cricket, when the ground is still slightly wet and reduces the bounce of the ball in an unpredictable way and so makes the game much more difficult, the batting side is said to be on a STICKY WICKET – a phrase now used to describe any difficult situation.

As cities grew in the industrial revolution wood was at a premium and any branches that fell down would be picked up and used as firewood. It would only be in the countryside, where there were still a lot of trees and relatively few people, that such sticks would be left around on the ground. Hence such areas were referred to by city dwellers as THE STICKS.

Well, I never knew that . . .
. . . 19th-century 'coffin ships' are connected to gym shoes

During the 16th century Italian bankers from Lombardy in Italy who had set up business in the City of London established themselves as sources of insurance for risky merchant expeditions. The street where many of them were based was named after them, and LOMBARD STREET became a popular area for merchants to meet.

In the 1690s one of the newfangled coffee shops in the City of London became popular with merchants and was soon the centre of news, gossip and insurance transactions for the shipping industry. Its popularity made it very cramped, and as there was no control over who could come in and conduct business some frauds took place. To overcome this the owner of the coffee shop decided to move premises and to make it a rule that anyone who wanted access to the trading part of the establishment had to become a member. Nowadays the business is a massive global concern, but the name of the establishment has remained that of the founder to this day – LLOYD'S OF LONDON, from Edward Lloyd's original 'Lloyd's Coffee Shop'.

One of the more common tricks perpetrated by ship owners was to deceive insurers about the size and state of their ships. By the end of the 19th century a practice had developed of purposely loading too much cargo onto old ships so that they would sink in poor weather, enabling the owner to claim on insurance. As the crew would be at serious risk of dying, these ships were called 'coffin ships'. Britain was the centre of the worldwide shipping insurance market, and so a British politician introduced a system to prevent the overloading. This measure, which formed part of the Merchant Shipping Act, involved painting a series of lines on the side of every ship to show where the waterline should be when the ship was fully loaded. The different lines were needed because of variations in the buoyancy of water: for example, the warm water of the tropics is less buoyant than the cold water of the North Atlantic in winter. The lines were named after the politician who sponsored the measure, Samuel Plimsoll. Hence we have the PLIMSOLL LINE, still used to this day.

Within a few years a new form of footwear was developed, incorporating a rubber sole which rose a little way up the side of the shoe to provide some protection when walking through shallow puddles. These shoes also became known as PLIMSOLLS.

To protect themselves against unknowingly insuring ships that were unseaworthy, Lloyd's created a list of ships with all key details agreed and audited. A derivation of this list is still used today and is called THE LLOYD'S SHIPPING LIST. All the ships listed were classified according to a letter, and within each letter by a number. The safest category of ships was given a reference that is nowadays used much more widely to describe 'the best' of anything: A1.

One difficulty for ships was barnacles that would grow on the underside of the hull. This would slow the ship down due to friction and could result in other parasites that would eat the wood away. Hence ships needed to be occasionally beached or put into dry dock to have the barnacles removed. To overcome this problem, later ships had the section of the hull that was under water covered in thin copper plates, to which barnacles could not attach themselves. This made the ships faster and of course more durable and safer. To be classified as A1 by Lloyd's, it was necessary to provide proof that your ship was protected in this way. Hence the phrase COPPER-BOTTOMED GUARANTEE.

As providing insurance for merchant ships became more commonplace, different groups of insurers adopted different standard terms and conditions. These basic rules, conditions and policies were set out in their standard documents, around which detailed adjustments could then be made for each case.

Hence we call them insurance POLICY DOCUMENTS. Once these terms had been agreed, the person authorized to act on behalf of the insurer would sign his name under the wording of the policy to indicate final approval of it. These people became known as UNDERWRITERS.

In 1793 at the coastal battle of Toulon a young Napoleon Bonaparte was captain of a battery of artillery trying to sink an attacking British fleet. A French frigate called the *Lutine* was captured by the British. Six years later she sank in the North Sea while carrying a cargo of gold and silver bullion. Some of the money was recovered, together with her rudder and bell. The rudder was made into a chair and the bell hung in the Lloyd's building to remind people of the financial risks they were involved in. The bell was then rung whenever a ship sank, or to gain attention before any important announcement – a tradition that continues to this day. It was called THE LUTINE BELL.

4

Knights and the English Longbow

Normally we don't like talking about violence, so you may be surprised to learn how many phrases we use casually in passing have their origins in the bloody conflicts of the past.

Well, I never knew that . . .

. . . a feather in your cap is real panache

In the Middle Ages, as knights tried to outdo each other with their finery, they used large dramatic feathers from exotic foreign birds to make themselves look resplendent. One such crest was that of John of Bohemia, who was defeated by Edward the Prince of Wales at the Battle of Crécy in 1346. Edward's father awarded this crest to the prince for his bravery – and the three ostrich feathers remain the crest of the Prince of Wales to this day. This crest was emblazoned upon a black background, and so the prince, who was known as a terrifyingly brave and bold fighter with no regard for his own safety in battle, came to be known as the BLACK PRINCE. His father, Edward III, created a new title based upon the Latin word for 'leader' specifically for his son. Subsequently, slightly over 20 such titles have been awarded and it remains the highest noble rank in Britain. It was called DUKE, from *dux* – Latin for leader. Incidentally, the only new dukedom in the 20th century was created when Philip was made Duke of Edinburgh in 1947. Unusually, at the start of the 20th century, the daughter of the dead Duke of Fife was made a duchess in her own right – the Duchess of Fife. Thus we get the Cockney slang for wife, DUCHESS (of Fife).

The king's award of feathers for bravery in battle then translated into a phrase used more widely to congratulate anyone who has achieved something notable: A FEATHER IN YOUR CAP. Indeed, over time, feathers have been awarded to whole regiments for their bravery and have been incorporated

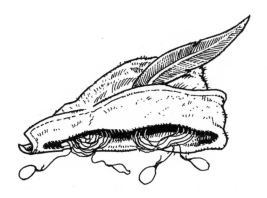

into the uniform, often the helmet. These items are named after the French word for feather, *plume,* from where we also get the word for feathers on a bird, PLUMAGE. In many regiments these plumes are the natural white. However, some regiments have conducted themselves with exceptional bravery in battles where they have either suffered tremendous casualties or inflicted severe casualties against an enemy who outnumbered them. These plumes are red, or half-red, as if dipped in blood.

The Italian word for a feather, *penna*, gives us the name for short, hollow tubes of pasta cut on the slant, PENNE, and the modern form of a quill, PEN. It was also used to describe the plume on the top of a knight's helmet that would add colour, make him more noticeable and give a flourish to his movements. This has given us the word for the quality of making a flourish in a social situation: PANACHE.

Authors often write under assumed names, which are called PEN NAMES – the names used when writing with a pen. As quills used to be made from feathers, or *plumes* in French, we get the old version of a pen name, NOM DE PLUME – literally, 'name of the feather'. At a distance the smoke from a fire can appear like a feather blowing in the breeze; hence the phrase A PLUME OF SMOKE.

Well, I never knew that . . .
. . . ribbons, sexy women and Georgian windows
are all connected

The word *bugan* (with a silent 'g'), meaning 'to bend', has given us the name of a weapon consisting of a thin bent pole: BOW. Someone who made things by cutting and then bending wood, such as bows or barrels made of curved staves, was called a BOWYER. The same meaning has given us the description of a feature in many Georgian houses, the BOW WINDOW, and a piece of material bent upon itself many times, A BOW RIBBON. Also, the bending of light that takes place when the sun shines on raindrops, creating curved bands of colour in the sky, is called a RAINBOW. The bending under strain of a shelf or a bridge is called BENDING AND BOWING, and the gesture to indicate deference to a social superior is BOWING. This linkage of the word *bugan* with a servant's willingness to do work for their superior led to the creation of another word, 'bugsome', meaning someone with high levels of energy. This soon became used to describe someone in good health and ultimately to a healthy-looking figure. This was increasingly applied to the figures of attractive full-bodied women as BUXOM.

Well, I never knew that . . .
. . . if a boss-eyed man cocked up he would probably fall short

The medieval knights had ruled society and the battlefield for over two hundred years when a new, longer version of the standard bow emerged on the battlefield. For the first time it gave arrows the power to penetrate even plate armour. They were usually six inches taller than the bowman, and so were called LONGBOWS. Originally developed by the Welsh in their guerrilla warfare against the English, this weapon killed many English knights. However, Welsh resistance was eventually subdued by Edward I through ruthless campaigning and a phenomenal castle-building campaign that resulted in Wales having, to this day, more castles per square mile than any other region in the world. In fact, this was the biggest building project the medieval world ever saw. As Wales was absorbed into England the Welsh archers were absorbed into the English army. So when the English army went north to fight the Scots in the 13th century, the deadly Welsh archers went with them. The Scottish soldiers had small round shields called 'targes', which offered little protection against the longbow, and the Scottish army led by Robert the Bruce was massacred. The archers had to practise every day to maintain the musculature and skills necessary to use the longbow, and so they used these captured shields to aim at, giving us the word TARGET.

Archery targets were often set up on bales of straw to make the centre of the target the height of a man's chest. The old English word for something firm to put something else on was *bas*, which gives us the modern word BASE. A slightly different pronunciation resulted in the base of the target being called a 'boss'. If an archer misjudged the distance and the arrow fell low, hitting this base, he was referred to as BOSS-EYED. If the arrow failed even to reach the boss, it was said to have FALLEN SHORT.

The English next used the longbow against the French at the battles of Poitiers, Crécy and Agincourt, decimating the French nobility. This was despite being outnumbered, half-starved, and exhausted from weeks of forced marching. The French, stubbornly refusing to accept that peasants could be so dangerous, suffered defeat after defeat at their hands.

Countless numbers of the French nobility were slaughtered, so whenever archers were captured they would have the first two fingers of their right hand cut off. These were the fingers used to pull the bowstring back, and without them the man could not fire the powerful bow. Hence before a battle the English archers would show that they had the capability and the intention to slaughter the French nobility by giving THE TWO-FINGERED SALUTE. The archers would then quickly seek a blessing of good luck and protection from evil by laying one finger 'across' another to form the shape of a cross, and so today we still CROSS OUR FINGERS for luck.

Arrows have three feathers (or fletches), and the slot in the end where the bowstring goes is carefully cut such that there is one fletch to one side and two (at an angle) on the other. It is important that the side with two angled fletches is the side that touches the bow so that the fletches are not distorted when the arrow is shot. In the heat of battle archers would pick an arrow and, holding their bow slightly sideways, quickly bring the arrow down onto their hand, then straighten up and shoot. Archers used to imagine a mark where they wanted the arrow to hit. If they were off to one side they would be WIDE OF THE MARK. It was important that they could quickly and accurately load their bows correctly and so the fletch that was on its own was differentiated by being from a darker cock goose instead of the lighter plumage of the hen goose. When an archer undergoing training got it the wrong way around, he would be told : 'No – COCK UP!'

Hence our phrase describing a mistake. Interestingly, this practice of getting the cock feather pointing upwards led to the word 'cock' being associated with 'upright'. Hence a hat with two or three corners of the brim turned up was called A COCKED HAT, and pulling up the hammer of a gun ready to fire it, COCKING the gun. The fairground game of throwing a hoop over a rod sticking up from the ground to win a chicken – and celebrating winning it – was called COCK A HOOP!

Records show that Henry V had over six million arrows with his army at the Battle of Agincourt. His archers frequently used them all up and then had to run out and retrieve them from the dead and wounded to re-use them. With a firing rate of one arrow every five seconds, by the time the first arrow had hit its target there would be two more in the air behind it and another in the bow of each archer ready to fire. A mass volley would blot out the sky and the darkness and the sound would scare the horses – not to mention the common soldiers – as the arrows came THICK AND FAST. The sheer number of arrows involved was staggering, and as each arrow needed three fletches or goose feathers, geese would regularly be plucked several times each year, even during cold weather. When plucked, the fowl's skin would react in the same way to the cold as human skin, but much more visibly: hence our phrase GOOSE PIMPLES.

Bowstrings were crucial and every archer had several in case one snapped in battle, or was exposed to rain, whereupon it would expand, losing all power and rendering the bow useless. Thus an archer needed – literally – to HAVE SEVERAL STRINGS TO HIS BOW.

The special knot used by archers for the loop at each end of the bowstring was called the BOWLINE knot.

Hoods and caps of various types were commonplace in medieval times and archers would often keep a spare bowstring under their hoods for easy and swift access during a battle. In fact, being superstitious, an archer would keep what he considered to be his 'lucky' bowstring there as a special reserve – KEEPING IT UNDER HIS HAT. This was a crucial element of the Battle of Crécy when a heavy rain shower moistened the strings of both the English longbows and the French crossbows. The strings stretched and this significantly reduced their power. However, the English simply replaced them with dry strings from under their hats and regained the full power of their longbows. The French crossbowmen did not and so quickly lost the arrow fight and ran away. This in turn prompted the French knights to charge the English archers by galloping straight through the 'cowardly' retreating crossbowmen, killing many more as they did so. That's chivalry for you!

The Greek word for a bow and anything associated with it was *toxon*. A practice in the early ancient Greek world was to apply magic potions or poison to arrows, and over time this led to the word being associated with poisons: so we have TOXINS and TOXIC. Also, from using the Greek word meaning 'into', we get the idea of ingesting a poison and suffering the consequences, although nowadays this is usually applied to substances that provide pleasurable feelings as well: INTOXICATED. Interestingly, the official name for archery is still TOXOPHILY.

St Sebastian was killed in the 3rd century by being tied to a tree and shot by many archers. Hence he is patron saint of ARCHERS – and, from his appearance after death, also patron saint of pin-makers! Edmund, King of Anglia in the 9th century, was also captured by Vikings, tied to a tree, and killed by archers. He is known as the 'English St Sebastian' and his remains are buried at his manor, St Edmunds Burgh, better known today as BURY ST EDMUNDS. Incidentally the 'bury' is a variation of 'burgh', meaning fortified place – no connection with his having been buried there!

Archers often used a small round shield that could be clipped to their belt or be held by a central grip. This grip would be protected by a small hemispherical metal protector called the shield boss. In French this was called a *boucle* and over time the shield became known to Englishmen as a BUCKLER. A

similar, though smaller, piece of metal was used to provide an impressive central feature on a knight's belt, and also served to secure the two ends of the belt together as a BUCKLE.

One form of practising field archery was to aim at trees or other natural targets while walking through the countryside. This became known by a term that means wandering with a purpose, but with no particular destination in mind: ROVING. A specific use of this word has developed, whereby a young man travelling and randomly looking around a new village might consciously try to spot a pretty local girl who might respond to his advances: A ROVING EYE. Such travellers would often have dogs with them, from which we get a common name for a dog: ROVER.

Making an arrow would involve several craftsmen, who have left their skills enshrined in the surnames that are still common today. The tree-cutter was a WOODMAN; shaping the wood to a rough bow shape was done by a CARPENTER; the bow was made by a BOWYER. Putting the feathers onto the arrows was done by a FLETCHER. The blacksmith who made the arrow heads was a SMITH, and the person who sharpened the arrow heads a POINTER.

The best longbows were very skilfully carved from yew, with the springy sapwood on the back of the bow and the less flexible reddish 'heartwood' on the outside. This provided maximum tension as the outside was stretched and the inside compressed. This is why yew bows are pale cream in the front and a deep red behind. The best yew came from the Mediterranean as it had fewer knots and imperfections – crucial if you are going to be putting great stresses and strains onto the device. England realized the strategic importance of this resource and so put a levy on all English boats trading internationally: they had to bring back Mediterranean yew and were not allowed to unload until they had first handed over the prized wood to the local officials!

The bows themselves were tailor-made for each archer, to just the right length, thickness and therefore stiffness for each individual. This stiffness is called the 'pull' or 'weight' of the bow. Longbows found in the *Mary Rose* have a 'pull' far greater than any modern-day archer could handle. This strength was achieved through years of constant practice and strengthening of back, arm and hand muscles from the age of around seven. This preparation was considered such a key part of national security that a law was passed banning another popular Sunday game in which a pig's bladder was inflated and then kicked or carried between two villages across the countryside: FOOTBALL. This law has never been repealed! Marksmen would also ideally choose individual arrows for length and thickness: the length to match their pull and the thickness to match the power of the bow. Otherwise the arrows would distort, flex in the air, and not fly true.

Well, I never knew that . . .
. . . a hawk's chin led to aggravating comments

There were different-shaped arrow heads for different purposes. There were thin, narrow ones called bodkins, named after bodkin 'pins', that were designed to 'punch' through armour. There were also cruel-looking ones with

backward-facing points, designed to injure horses. *Barba* is Latin for 'beard' – from where we get the word BARBER – and was used in medieval times to describe the rearward-pointing tip of a hawk's beak that vaguely resembled the pointed beard of a man. Hence the sharp backward-facing points on arrows were also called BARBS. When these barbed arrows penetrated a horse's flank they would not fall out, but instead would gradually tear the muscles and open the wound up further as the horse moved around, causing more pain and distraction. This idea of penetrating and causing a significant, annoying and continuing hurt has led to the phrase A BARBED COMMENT.

Ironically, the archers were themselves a key cause of the decline in use of the longbow on battlefields. This was because during the Hundred Years War they returned from France inadvertently bringing with them rats carrying the Black Death. This decimated the population by some 50% in London and 30% elsewhere in Britain. This, in turn, caused a massive shortage of manpower and it became impractical to dedicate so much time to archery practice. Instead, a new invention from China offered a weapon that took much less physical specialization and skill to use: GUNPOWDER and GUNS. It has been assessed that a regiment of 14th-century archers would have beaten a similar-sized regiment of musketeers up until the late 19th century, when repeating rifles appeared in the American Civil War.

Incidentally, you cannot 'fire' a bow – because no fire is involved. You can fire a gun because originally you applied a burning flame (fire) to the gunpowder. You 'shoot' an arrow from a bow.

Well, I never knew that . . .
. . . shooting an arrow straight at a white dot
defines close range

In medieval France, archery targets were painted blue with a white spot in the middle. English archers were more accurate and added a small red central dot. This was named after a farm animal as the BULLSEYE. The range at which an archer

could HIT THE WHITE dot at the centre of the French target with a direct straight shot without needing to arc the shot up is what we call POINT BLANK range, from *point blanc*, meaning white dot. Also, to ask a very *direct* question designed to address the heart of an issue is to 'ask the question point blank'. The English equivalent to this phrase is TO HIT THE WHITE – meaning on target.

Well, I never knew that ...
... once you have shot your bolt you may well
become the quarry

A different form of bow consisted of a central piece of wood with the bow secured near to one end, creating a cross-shape; this was called a CROSSBOW. The arrows used were much shorter than the arrows used for longbows and in comparison resembled the short, stubby iron rods used to keep a door securely closed. Hence these arrows were called CROSSBOW BOLTS. Crossbows were much easier to use than longbows and required less skill and technique. The disadvantage was that they took a long time to load, sometimes several minutes. Hence if a crossbowman was facing an attacking knight, he would probably only get one chance to fire his short arrow called a bolt, whereas a longbowman would have several attempts. From this comes the phrase SHOT HIS BOLT, meaning having used his only chance.

If a horse takes fright and suddenly gallops away, it can shoot off very fast – like the speed of a crossbow arrow – hence we say it has BOLTED.

When a longbow is fired at a distant target, it must be aimed high to allow for the weight of the long arrow. However, a crossbow bolt is lighter and is fired with much more power, enabling the marksman to aim directly at his intended target. Hence there was an old saying AS STRAIGHT AS A BOLT. Over time this turned into a different saying, meaning sitting up straight: BOLT UPRIGHT.

The crossbow arrows were typically made with a short arrowhead with a square (*quadrus* in Latin) cross-section, designed to punch its way through armour. Hence the alternative name for a crossbow bolt: a QUARREL. When stone was mined in the Middle Ages for building churches,

cathedrals, and castles, it would often be cut into rough squares just after being taken from the ground, and then transported semi-finished. Hence the name for these areas: QUARRIES, from *quadrare*, meaning to make square. Coincidentally, the old French word *cuirée*, meaning 'skinned', is the source of our word for an animal being hunted, because its skin would be given to the hunting dogs after the humans took the meat. Its spelling has changed over time to QUARRY.

5

Food and Drink

How and what we eat and drink
have changed beyond recognition
over the centuries – but words we
use without thinking today remind
us of the days when getting a meal
on the table took a lot more than a
trip to the supermarket.

Well, I never knew that . . .
. . . shopkeepers take such a big cut because
they are so engrossing

T he word 'species' was originally applied by the Greeks to differentiate between types of animals. Later the word was also adapted to describe the new varieties of 'hot' roots and vegetables that were being imported into Europe from the east during the Middle Ages: SPICES. These spices livened up the boring English dishes of the time and this analogy was applied to other aspects of life, which is why we SPICE SOMETHING UP. Spices became big business in France, where the word was used to describe the growing wealth of traders in these goods and other foods, giving the French word still used for such people – *épicier*. In England the money was being made by the importers, who bought *whole* cargoes and *sold* them on in smaller quantities: WHOLESALERS. Many items would be packed twelve to a box, and the wholesaler would order twelve of these boxes at a time to send to different shopkeepers. This large (*grossus* in Latin) wholesale quantity, totalling 144 items, was therefore called A GROSS. Over the years these traders, and eventually the smaller shopkeepers whom they supplied, became known as GROCERS, again from *grossus*. When such a trader bought up an entire shipment in one deal it was described with a word that we still use to this day: ENGROSSED, meaning to have a complete obsession with one thing. By the time the goods had reached a shop the quantities had been split or cut several times, and the shopkeeper would 'cut' them yet again into individual items for sale to the public. Using the Latin word *taliare* (from which we also get the name for a clothes-maker or TAILOR), we get the alternative name for shopkeepers: re-taliares or RETAILERS.

Well, I never knew that . . .
. . . thrashing around saved Second World War
bombers and modern jet fighters

A basic requirement of farming is to find a way of extracting the nutritious wheat germ from the rest of the plant called the chaff. Hence the phrase meaning to identify the best people from a wider mixed group of abilities: SEPARATE THE WHEAT FROM THE CHAFF.

An old practice of stamping on harvested wheat with wooden-soled shoes to help separate the nutritious ears from the stalks is named after an old Germanic word, *threshing*, meaning 'to stamp'. The stalks were referred to as 'thresh', and used as doormats to reduce the amount of mud being brought into houses. A plank of wood was placed at the opening to 'hold' these stalks in place: hence we get the word THRESHOLD.

Another variant is derived from when flails were introduced, with heavy sections of wood chained together, to strike the wheat, but is now used in a wider sense: TO THRASH. This idea has also led to an expression meaning to separate out the key points of a difficult situation from other less important parts and hence agree a solution: TO THRASH OUT AN IDEA. Also, the image of repeatedly exerting oneself with physical activity has been applied to people who move jerkily, perhaps in pain: THRASHING AROUND.

When threshing used to be done by hand the husks would appear as a small cloud blowing in the wind, which would to some extent obscure vision until it had drifted away. Hence when a product was developed, made of thin strips of metal foil, to be dropped from the air to confuse radar in the Second World War, it was, and still is, called CHAFF.

Well, I never knew that . . .
. . . you need a pot shot to have pot luck!

Peasant food was very seasonal and in bad times they would have to improvise. Typically, a cooking pot would be kept stewing over a fire and whatever was available was put in. This would then be served out by ladle at mealtimes. Hence the phrase referring to what you may get on your plate: POT LUCK. If someone went out into the woods to kill an animal for food without caring too much what the animal actually was, they would take a POT SHOT, meaning it didn't matter what they hit. If they did shoot something, or if

they selected an animal from the farmyard, it would be ONE
FOR THE POT.

If food was short and it was necessary to eat an old goat
or sheep whose meat would be tough, it would usually be
cut up into small portions and then boiled in the pot for a
long time. The animal was said to have GONE TO POT. Using
the analogy of cutting up tough or otherwise poor-quality
meat into very small pieces so that it is easier to chew
and then swallow, a phrase has also developed meaning to
make a difficult message easier to accept, although this is

usually used in the negative: DON'T MINCE YOUR WORDS. The idea of being cut up into little pieces by being severely reprimanded also gives us the phrase BEING PUT THROUGH THE MINCER.

Well, I never knew that . . .
. . . brokers have no problem broaching their favourite subject

Broche was an old French word for a sharp tool used to pierce thick cloth, for example in sail-making. From this idea we get the word for an item of jewellery that is fastened to clothes by piercing with a sharp pin: a BROOCH. In turn this led to a new word in the English language meaning to pierce: BROACH.

Barrels of ale and wine have a small hole sealed with a wooden plug. To access the contents a specially shaped hollow peg, with a valve on it, is hammered in, replacing the wooden plug and allowing the ale to be drawn off. The peg has two names. One is the 'broach'. From this process of banging the broach into the barrel we get 'broaching the barrel' which, in turn, gives us a phrase for introducing a sensitive topic into a conversation BROACHING A SUBJECT. The second name comes from the way it was inserted, by gently hitting the end of the peg with a mallet. This gives us the term for such a tube with a controllable valve, a TAP, and the process of letting the drink run out into bottles, TAPPING IT OFF. Men who bought barrels of wine, broached them to taste the contents, and then sold the wine on, either in barrels or sometimes in bottles, have given us the term BROKERS, from 'broacher'. This then came to apply to wholesalers of any commodity when the relevant word was added in front – as, for example, in DIAMOND BROKER or MORTGAGE BROKER.

Well, I never knew that . . .

. . . the French go on and on in the English language

A cut of beef from just above the loin takes its name from the French description, although one letter has subsequently changed to give its modern spelling: SIRLOIN, from *sur loin* – above the loin. The rumour that some king was so impressed with the flavour that he knighted the loin and made it Sir Loin is an amusing but fanciful story. Another use of *sur* is when something forms a circle *around* an item of interest: SURROUND. A subtly different use of the French word *sur* is where 'on top' means 'more of', as opposed to physically above: thus to have more of life is to SURVIVE, from *vivre* (to live), and more than enough is a SURPLUS.

The Old English word *creodan* meaning 'to be forced together' has given us three words. The first describes coagulating milk that floats to the surface and can then be used to make cheese: CURD. The second is the name given to the bits of dirt and muck that used to collect inside a suit of armour during a day's battle, resulting in a nasty congealed mess. Nowadays it is used in a wider and often less unpleasant sense: CRUD. Lastly, when a lot of people congregate together, we have a CROWD.

Well, I never knew that . . .
. . . there is so much salt in our food we can't leave it alone

In Victorian days there would often be a large silver salt cellar for everyone to use, and so this would be placed in the centre of the table. Special guests would expect to be seated near their host – certainly on the half of the table nearest their host – hence the phrase for being in the best company: TO SIT ABOVE THE SALT.

Salt was considered to be a purifying substance and could protect against tainted or even poisonous food, so that if you were unsure about some food you had eaten you would take and eat a small amount of salt to ensure that it had no effect: TAKE IT WITH A PINCH OF SALT, meaning don't worry about the potential danger. An exaggerated version of this saying is TAKE IT WITH A GRAIN OF SALT. Some people would throw a pinch of salt over their shoulder on the basis that the purity of the salt would ward off evil spirits.

The Romans loved eating vegetables and leaves with dressings and lots of salt. In fact they called such dishes *herba salata*, meaning salted herbs, from which we get the phrase GREEN SALAD. A particular fruity and salty dressing based on tomatoes was called SALSA. A salted and spicy pork sausage was called SALAMI. And even our word SAUSAGE is ultimately derived from Latin *salsicia*, referring to salted pork. Salt was also used as a preservative, either rubbed into meat, such as pork, or as a brine solution. From this we get the phrase meaning to store something away for the future: to SALT IT AWAY.

6

Ancient Greek Mythology

We're used to looking back to
classical Greece in politics, art,
literature and philosophy – but the
weather? Look at the language and
you'll see how much more they
left us.

Well, I never knew that . . .
. . . it is so easy to make someone look
devilishly horny in a photograph

In ancient Greek mythology there was a hundred-headed monster who would whirl around causing death and destruction. Its name was used to describe very fierce storms and has subsequently been used to name several generations of well-armed attack aircraft: TYPHOON. Pan, the son of the Greek gods, lived in woods and forests where he was constantly making amorous moves on the nymphs who also lived in the woods. One such nymph, whose singing enchanted him, escaped him by turning into reeds by a lake. But Pan cut down the reeds and made pipes from them: PAN-PIPES. Whenever humans came through the forests he would scare them away by shouting and making scary noises to protect 'his' nymphs, causing PANIC. One day Typhoon was chasing after Pan, who escaped by disguising himself as a goat (*caper* in Greek) with horns (*cornu*). In this form he became known as CAPRICORN. Zeus, the king of the gods, subsequently made him into one of the SIGNS OF THE

ZODIAC. Unfortunately, Pan could never fully reverse the disguise, hence his horns and goat's legs.

The ram-headed Amon was the Egyptian god of fertility. This led to similar associations throughout history, including the horned satyrs of Greece, and gave us the slang term HORNY. As the Christian church tried to turn people away from their old pagan gods, they associated such images of previously worshipped deities with evil and wrongdoing; hence the traditional appearance of THE DEVIL as a horned and cloven-hoofed sexual predator. A simple representation of these two horns is also the source of the juvenile gesture when someone raises two fingers behind the head of someone else – for example, when a photograph is being taken.

Greek mythology tells of the dryads who live inside trees and offer advice and good luck blessings to people who knock gently on the bark of the tree. Hence the phrases KNOCK ON WOOD and TOUCH WOOD, meaning wishing for good luck.

Zeus liked to frolic with dryads. To keep his wife Hera away, he used one of the dryads to distract her. When Hera found out she cursed the dryad so that she would never be able to speak again, other than to repeat the words others said to her. The dryad then saw a very beautiful young man staring constantly at his own reflection in the water, admiring his own beauty to such an extent he did not notice anything else. From his name, Narcissus, we get the word to describe someone who is self-obsessed: NARCISSISTIC. His self-obsession and her curse resulted in the dryad eventually wasting away due to her unrequited love for the boy, until all that was left was her voice. Her name was ECHO. Incidentally, the boy's obsession with his own beauty led the gods to punish him by turning him into a flower, the NARCISSUS. When it was discovered that some of these plants contain chemicals that can be used to create euphoria and then sleep, the chemicals were called NARCOTICS.

In Greek mythology a traveller passing through a forest in winter is befriended by a grumpy satyr who offers to help and provides some piping hot food for the cold man. The traveller blows on his hands to warm them and then blows on the hot food to cool it down. At this, the satyr complains that he is implying his dissatisfaction with his hospitality, saying that it is both too hot and too cold in the same breath, and throws him out again into the cold weather! Hence we get the phrase BLOWING HOT AND COLD.

When Zeus was born his mother hid him in a cave so that his father Kronos could not eat him – his normal way of ensuring no son could threaten him later in life! A goat fed him milk, and bees fed him honey. In addition, a horn (*cornu* in Latin) was broken off the goat and this was magically refilled every day with fruit and herbs. The Roman word for plenty is *copia*, from which we get the word meaning abundant, COPIOUS. In English this magical horn was called the HORN OF PLENTY – still offered as a dessert in some restaurants – or, in Latin, *cornucopia*.

Well, I never knew that . . .
. . . one of the world's most famous statues to sexy love – isn't!

Eros was the son of Aphrodite, the Greek goddess of love, who had the power to make others desire her uncontrollably.

We call a food or drink or drug that has this effect an APHRODISIAC. Eros had the perfect physique and was exceptionally sexually attractive, and he too had many partners; so we call someone who is very desirable EROTIC. Areas of the body that stimulate sexual desire are called EROGENOUS ZONES.

Aphrodite's husband was Hephaestos, the blacksmith of the gods, and the god of fire and molten metal. The Romans called him Vulcan, from which we get the word for heat-treated rubber, VULCANIZED RUBBER, and for a mountain that ejects molten rock, VOLCANO.

The Romans had exactly the same story, with Venus being the equivalent of Aphrodite. Again the goddess had many lovers, so that we get from her name the phrase for diseases associated with a lot of sexual activity: VENEREAL DISEASES. Cupid was the Roman equivalent of Eros. His mother's amorous activities embarrassed him so much that he had a rose blessed by Harpocrates, the god of silence, such that anyone whom Cupid touched with the rose was unable to talk of their conquest of his mother. The rose subsequently became a symbol of secrecy in the ancient world and over the centuries a tradition developed that if a rose was hung from the ceiling, anything that was said in that room was considered to be said in confidence and not to be repeated. Hence the use of the Latin phrase for 'under the rose' to mean confidential: *SUB ROSA*. This is why Catholic confessionals and

banqueting halls have roses either carved in the ceiling or moulded in the plaster, to signify that any discussion there is automatically confidential. This is why such plaster embellishments or pseudo-plaster castings on ceilings are called CEILING ROSES – even if they are not roses!

In 1893 the 7th Earl of Shaftesbury, a wealthy Christian philanthropist, had a fountain and a statue of the Angel of Christian Charity installed at the end of the road named after him, SHAFTESBURY AVENUE. The Earl designed a pun into the statue. The figure was shooting a bow such that the arrow ('shaft') would land and 'bury' itself in the road that he had also had built. However, when the statue was described as the angel of love (referring to God's love), it was popularly and erroneously misinterpreted as referring to the Greek god of love, EROS – as it is still known throughout the world! It was originally designed as the centre of the roundabout in Piccadilly Circus, with a water fountain and drinking trough, and with the statue appearing to stand on the top of the gushing water. However, town planners insisted on a smaller base, which meant that the water splashed out, and before long the fountain was turned off. Then the original aluminium statue was replaced with a lead copy that now faces away from Shaftesbury Avenue! There isn't even a roundabout there any more! Still, while the statue is very different from how it was originally planned, it does remain a key London landmark.

Well, I never knew that . . .
. . . when hot-blooded people get fired up they
can make other people's blood run cold

Candere was the Latin word for shining or glowing. Hence we get the word for anything that glows in the dark, INCANDESCENT, and items manufactured to light the darkness, CANDLES. Several candles together on one decorative item make up a CANDELABRUM. A larger collection of candles to light large rooms takes its name from the French word for candle, *chandelle*: a CHANDELIER. A closely related derivation also gives rise to the word for a glowing aromatic stick, INCENSE. From when these wicks have been soaked in herbs or drugs of various forms, giving some form of narcotic effect, we get the word meaning to be inspired without keeping full self-control, INCENSED, and also the idea of providing a very clear reason for someone to strive harder because their passion or desire has been set on fire, INCENTIVE. The link with burning also gives the name for bombs specifically made to create fires: INCENDIARY BOMBS.

The medieval peoples thought that the temperature of blood dictated one's mood and behaviour. Someone driven by passion and emotion was HOT-BLOODED, and to avoid taking an action that they might later regret would be advised by friends to COOL OFF. Indeed, this phrasing still exists in many contracts where there are a number of days after signing during which you can cancel if, in hindsight, you believe your emotions overrode your logic at the time of signing: a

COOLING-OFF PERIOD. Anyone who planned a dastardly act without caring for the victim at all would be considered COLD-BLOODED. Someone who was less extreme but still unfriendly would be considered COLD. Hence there was an association between heat and desire. At the level of physical attraction you can say that you HAVE THE HOTS for someone. In the 17th century the high water content of cucumbers meant they became associated with cooling emotions down, and prudish women would often be referred to as 'cold as a cucumber', which over time has become 'COOL AS A CUCUMBER', nowadays meaning in control and unflustered. The reference to heat gives us the phrase to describe someone who has become very enthusiastic and energetic as FIRED UP, and the idea of infuriating someone to the point of SETTING THEIR EMOTIONS ON FIRE. This notion of heat and fire making one's blood bubble with emotion has also given us the phrase for someone who is so frustrated that their BLOOD IS BOILING, and that their rage means they can only SEE RED.

When someone is scared, adrenalin kicks in and blood is withdrawn from the extremities to be available for muscles and the important inner organs – the classic 'fight or flight' response. Hence the extremities go cooler and whiter. Friends may say you are as WHITE AS A SHEET or AS PALE AS A GHOST, or that you look AS IF YOU HAVE SEEN A GHOST. In olden days it was thought that the temperature of the blood actually fell when you were scared, MAKING YOUR BLOOD RUN COLD. Metaphorically, if someone is frightened about a proposed course of action and is markedly hesitant, they are said to be GETTING COLD FEET. While the blood does not actually get cooler, the extremities do feel colder as the blood flow is reduced. Also, we have the phrase MAKING YOUR BLOOD FREEZE.

7

Medieval Craftsmen

In medieval times every craft and
trade had its guild, complete with
apprenticeship system and specialist
terms. The economy has changed
out of all recognition since then –
but yet again the language retains
clues to the old practices.

Well, I never knew that . . .
. . . loving your work stops when you
make a masterpiece

From the Latin word *amor*, meaning to love, we get someone who loves to do something even if he is not fully trained or accredited or even very good at it: an AMATEUR, via *amator*. When an apprentice agreed to work for

a master to learn a craft, the pay was initially very low. But over time the apprentice would gain skills and be paid an increasing wage. This and other parts of the deal would be agreed and then written down as a legal document or deed.

This document would have the same agreement written out twice and then would be formally separated with jagged, zigzag cuts reminiscent of teeth-marks. From the Latin word for a tooth, *dens* (from which we get 'dentist'), these cuts came to be called INDENTATIONS. Each party would keep a copy. The

originals would then perfectly match each other if there was a dispute. Hence the word for the legal contractual document, an INDENTURE, and the word for such apprenticeships, INDENTURED labour or service. When a legal agreement was one-sided and therefore less contentious, there was no need for the jagged edge and so the document would be written on paper or parchment with a straight (or polled) edge. Hence they are called DEED POLLS. Changing your name is an example of how such a document is still used.

When an apprenticeship was satisfactorily completed, the former trainee would become a craftsman and could eventually apply to the guild to became a master craftsman. To do that he would need to submit a piece of work that would be examined by existing masters who would decide if it was good enough to justify the person becoming a master craftsman. The word for such a piece is still used in some areas such as clock-making, painting and cabinet-making, as well as more widely outside the classic craft areas: a MASTERPIECE.

Over the years it has become traditional for apprentices to be the butt of humiliating practical jokes. Stories abound of

the printer's apprentice asked to get a bottle of
STRIPED INK;

the office junior asked to get WHITE CARBON PAPER;

the trainee soldier asked to get a FIRING LINE;

the sailor who was put on watch to look out so that he
could warn the crew when the ship was about to
BUMP OVER THE EQUATOR;

the Royal Navy apprentice who was told to get milk for
the SEACAT (missile!);

the sailor told to go and UNLOCK DAVY JONES'S LOCKER;

the apprentice builder who was told to get a FOUR-FOOT
YARDSTICK;

the carpenter's apprentice who had to get a GLASS
MALLET;

the mason's apprentice who was told to keep a look out
for the SKY HOOKS;

the post office worker who was told to develop 'the
POST CODE FOR LIFE concept';

the painter's apprentice who was told to WATCH THE
GLOSS PAINT UNTIL IT HAD DRIED;

the computer apprentice who was told that, as he was
in training, INSTEAD OF GETTING A HARD DISK HE
SHOULD ASK FOR AN EASIER ONE;

the sailor who was told to check that THE PORT AND
STARBOARD WATCHES WERE IN TIME with each other;

the zookeeper's apprentice who was told to go and get
a CIRCLE OF LIFE;

the IT support apprentice who was told that IF A
CUSTOMER REPORTED A CRASHED PC THEY SHOULD
PHONE THE AA;

the trainee estate agent sent to a chandler's to get FOUR
SAIL SIGNS;

the tailor's apprentice who was told to get a HALF A
DOZEN BUTTON HOLES;

the architect's apprentice who was told always to
sketch the plans for water features using a
FOUNTAIN PEN;

the electrician's apprentice told to get a SHORT CIRCUIT;

the accountant told to get A CHAIR FOR THE INTEREST
TABLE.

Well, I never knew that . . .
. . . nailing the derivation of 'as dead as a door nail'
is a dead end

When nails are being hammered into place, if they come through the other side the ends can be hammered over to prevent them from slipping or being pulled out. When this happens they are said to be 'dead' – because they will not be reusable. However, in most applications the nails do not show through. Perhaps the most common application where they do was in the making of doors, where the extra strength to be gained by bending the ends over would be very valuable; hence AS DEAD AS A DOOR NAIL. This also gives us the idea of

completing a task as NAILING IT. A similar meaning of the word 'dead' is used to describe a bolt within the structure of a door that can only be moved into or out of position with a key. The sense here is that, once in place, the bolt is 'dead' to anyone without the key, as opposed to a lock with some form of handle that anyone can use; hence the more secure fastening is called a DEADLOCK – a word also used to describe an argument where no one can see a way of moving forward. Equally, as roads are often used as a metaphor for the journey of life, an alleyway that does not lead any where is called a DEAD END.

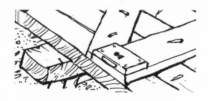

Well, I never knew that . . .
. . . 'getting the sack' is much better than 'being fired'!

Saq was originally a Middle Eastern word for a very rough material. The use of this material for basic bags gives us the word SACK. The use of such bags by Vikings and others to take away plunder gives us the additional meaning of the word: TO SACK a building or town. In medieval days craftsmen such as carpenters and masons would carry the tools of their trade with them in a bag as they travelled around looking for work. Hence when leaving the work-site after, for example, being dismissed, they would be GIVEN THE SACK. If they had acted

dishonestly or their workmanship had caused an injury to fellow workmen, their tools would be burnt so that they could not endanger others elsewhere at another building site. They would be FIRED.

The French name for a small bag that can be carried easily on one's shoulders has given us the word SATCHEL.

The Dutch word for a leather bag or bucket for carrying around tools was *kitte*. From this we get the word for the set of tools that a professional needs to do his job: KIT; also our term for such a bag that could be easily slung over his shoulder: KIT BAG. The idea of workers pooling their funds at meal times so that one of them can buy food and bring it back in their bag gives us the term for shared funds: KITTY. When a large job such as a cathedral was finished the workers would pick up their tools and all of their other possessions (*boedel* in Dutch) and move on to the next job. This gives us the phrase KIT AND CABOODLE.

8

Crime and Punishment

We may be upright, law-abiding
citizens, but hardly a day goes by
when we don't use the language of
the criminal underworld without
ever being aware of it – until now.

Well, I never knew that . . .
. . . dukes regularly appeared in fist fights with commoners

In the 19th century thieves drew an analogy between their 'sharp' fingers, which were skilled at removing items from a victim's pockets, and a fork used for picking up food from a plate to describe their activities as PICKING POCKETS. For many years thieves referred to fingers as 'forks'. Hence the phrase for picking money out of your own pocket and handing it over to someone else, FORKING OUT. Also, the Cockney rhyming slang to describe hands, DUKE OF YORKS (forks), gives us the term for fists used in a boxing match: DUKES, as in 'PUT YOUR DUKES UP'.

Well, I never knew that . . .
. . . being on the wagon is far worse than being
on the treadmill

In Victorian prisons there was strong emphasis on the punishment, as opposed to rehabilitation, of criminals. One diabolical device had a handle attached to a rotating metal wheel inside a metal box. The prisoner had to rotate the wheel several thousand times every day. This was backbreaking work and entirely unconstructive. In addition, the prison warder could adjust the friction on the wheel (and therefore the difficulty of turning it) by adjusting a screw with a special tool. Hence the nickname for a prison warder, SCREW, and the phrase for applying more pressure on someone, TURNING THE SCREW – and the phrase to describe someone suffering increased pressure or expense and not being able to do anything about it: BEING SCREWED.

Another form of punishment was being forced to walk on the inside of a rotating wooden wheel (like a giant hamster's wheel) for hours on end. Sometimes these wheels would be connected to machinery to take advantage of the energy, but often it was simply another form of exhausting and monotonous punishment – being put ON THE TREADMILL.

In medieval days, just before a sentenced criminal was taken from Newgate prison westwards towards Tyburn (now Marble Arch) to be executed, he would be offered a final drink – ONE FOR THE ROAD. However, once he mounted the cart that would

take him there on public display, he was not allowed anything more to drink. Hence the phrase meaning you've stopped taking alcohol: ON THE WAGON. The direction of the journey from Newgate to Tyburn has also given us the phrase GO WEST, meaning to die.

Well, I never knew that . . .
. . . keeping your eyes peeled is a fair cop

Up until the 19th century there was no respected public police force. Many towns employed nightwatchmen and some walled towns had gatekeepers, but the streets were often a no-go area at night and, in some areas, even during the day. While he was secretary for Ireland, Sir Robert Peel saw soldiers being used to police local communities with some degree of success, although the red uniforms reminded the locals of their submission to British rule and became a source of conflict, distrust and resentment. A decade later he established the Metropolitan Police Force in London, training them, giving them a uniform and paying them. The uniform was a blue jacket with copper buttons and a non-military hat.

This was specifically designed to differentiate its wearers from the rough red-coated soldiers of the day. People were very suspicious of them initially and several nicknames developed, including two named after the founder: BOBBIES (after Robert) and PEELERS, from his surname. The thin skin of our eyelids, which protects the eyeballs, had been likened to thin skin or peel on the outside of fruit. This, combined with the new nickname for policemen, gives us the phrase for keeping a lookout for wrongdoing, KEEPING YOUR EYES PEELED.

A famous cartoonist in the First World War created a friendly character called William – a soldier in the trenches with a big bushy moustache who became a popular household name.

After the war many ex-soldiers – who, incidentally, had been encouraged to grow moustaches to hide any trembling upper lip after suffering the horrendous conditions of the war, to help them keep a STIFF UPPER LIP – found many jobs difficult to find or keep, and a lot of them ended up in the growing police force. The name stuck, and so we now have the nickname OLD BILL.

From the French *capter* (to seize) we get the words for being arrested, COPPED, and for being caught out, COPPING IT. Also, when a criminal is caught red handed he may say : 'FAIR COP'.

This was then applied to the new policeman as a nickname: COPPER – one who cops criminals (although this was also a pun on the fact that the new uniform had copper buttons).

Since the 1860s low value coins have been made from bronze, but they are collectively still known by the original metal used, as COPPERS. As slot machines became popular and it was found that damaged coins would not work, the pun to describe a useless or dishonest policeman developed: BENT COPPER.

In the Middle Ages, Jews would often be tolerated as useful moneylenders for periods of time but then be persecuted by the King, usually in order to take money from them either as enforced loans or even as a permanent gift. Clearly the Jews would be reluctant to hand their money over and so they would often be pulled slowly over red-hot coals until they changed their minds: hence the phrase BEING HAULED OVER THE COALS. Alternatively they would be tied to a frame that was held over a fire. These frames could usually be lowered and raised to adjust the effect. Hence the phrase TO GET A ROASTING, or to be 'roasted'. In the 19th century the London

underworld began to use a similar-sounding word to describe being arrested, and then being given a tough interrogation or reprimand by the police: TO ROAST SOMEONE or TO GIVE SOMEONE A ROASTING. From here we get the 19th-century slang for policemen: ROZZERS.

Well, I never knew that . . .
. . . even clever people can be as thick as two short planks

The word 'thick' used to mean 'very close'. Hence the phrase referring to family ties: BLOOD IS THICKER THAN WATER. Also, as thieves around the world often congregate together and form very close-knit groups of mutual support, we get the phrase

AS THICK AS THIEVES. A similar use of this word, which nowadays is often misunderstood, was originally used to describe two people who are such good friends that they are as close to each other as the watertight seal on a ship's deck: AS THICK AS TWO SHORT PLANKS. (The planks used for the sides of the hull were longer than the short ones used on deck.)

Well, I never knew that . . .
. . . we teach our children how to smuggle in nursery school

In the 17th and 18th centuries tax collectors who collected the government's revenues came to be known as REVENUE MEN. Those who worked on the coast would try to find out where

smugglers were landing and then ambush them. However, the smugglers would always have men on the shore keeping an eye out for such ambushes and would only signal to the smugglers when they had checked that THE COAST WAS CLEAR, which usually meant that the revenue men were too late and had to follow them on land. In the heyday of smuggling in the 18th century the government started to use bloodhounds to track down smugglers. But the smugglers, who were often related to the fishermen, quickly discovered that they could put the bloodhounds off by dragging raw/cured/pickled fish over their tracks – laying A RED HERRING.

In the 18th and 19th centuries many great wheezes were developed to beat the revenue men's increasing determination to catch smugglers. One was to tie barrels full of contraband to a rope which was tied to the smugglers' boat. These were called 'tails' by the smugglers and would be dragged behind the boat. If approached by revenue men, the smugglers would simply cut the rope, whereupon the barrels would sink and no incriminating evidence would be found! The smugglers would then return to the location later and retrieve the barrels from the seabed with the aid of specially made hooks. In the Hastings area the smugglers were locally known as 'sheep' and the revenue men were compared to a naïve and bungling shepherdess who was always looking (peeping) for the smugglers but could not keep track of them, let alone catch them. A story is told, disguised as a nursery rhyme for children, about these smugglers and the bungling revenue men, even describing how, when the barrels are found, the smugglers are gone and the forces of the law cannot convict anyone:

> *Little Bo Peep has lost her sheep*
> *And doesn't know where to find them*
> *Leave them alone and they will come home*
> *Dragging their tails behind them*

Little Bo Peep fell fast asleep,
And dreamt she heard them bleating
But when she awoke she found it a joke
For they were still all fleeting

Then up she got and took her crook
Determined to find them
She found them indeed but it made her heart bleed
For they'd left their tails behind them.

It happened one day as Bo Peep did try
Into a meadow hard by,
There she espied their tails side by side,
All hung on a tree to dry.

She heaved a sigh and wiped her eye,
And over the hillocks went rambling,
And tried what she could, as a shepherdess would,
To tack again each to his lambkin –

– i.e. she couldn't get the evidence to prosecute.

Eventually the revenue men became so desperate to catch smugglers that they offered very substantial rewards for information, and this enticement did lead to some smugglers being captured and convicted. But these small local fishing communities were more like extended families and informing was considered an unforgivable betrayal, often leading to swift and violent death. Hence, these rewards became known as BLOOD MONEY.

9

London Cabbies

Think what you most associate with
the capital city and the things that
come to mind probably include royal
processions, magnificent architecture
. . . and traffic. If you thought
the word 'cab' was invented in
New York – think again!

Well, I never knew that . . .
. . . Cabbie! is a very hackneyed expression

In the late 1700s a new form of partially open-top horse-drawn carriage was designed in France, where it became very popular. It was two-wheeled and designed to carry a driver and two passengers under a protective hood. The suspension was designed to cope with the rough roads of the day and passengers remarked that, together with the motion

of the single horse that pulled it, its movement was a little like a young goat prancing around. A fully grown goat with horns, as in the astrological sign, is called Capricorn (*corn* meaning horn) as in the astrological sign. A young kid that has not grown any horns is called 'capri' or 'cabri'. Hence the carriage became known as a CABRIOLET. Many open-top cars today are still called cabriolet variants of the standard saloon.

In the early 1800s an inventor named Joseph Hansom improved the design of the original carriage by repositioning the driver behind the passenger compartment. This new design was called THE HANSOM CAB, or 'hansom' for short. In the early 20th century a motor car was designed for carrying paying customers around cities, and to differentiate it from a

hansom it used the old name, cabriolet, shortened to CAB. The drivers of this new carriage became known as CABBIES. At the same time an automated meter device for charging was introduced. This had been used in France for some time and so the English simply adopted the French term 'taximeter'. From this we got the name 'taximeter cabriolet' – soon shortened to TAXICAB and then just TAXI.

The French had bred a type of horse for pulling carriages called *haque-nays*. While this breed was not always used in the UK, the name became associated with the new cabriolets and was easily confused with the similar-sounding area of London where many cabbies lived; so the vehicles became

known as HACKNEY CABS. Many cab drivers were from the East End of London and the area of Hackney developed as the centre of stabling for cabbies' horses. These would often be hired by the day, worked very hard and left very tired. Hence the phrase implying that a set of words is overused and metaphorically very tired: A HACKNEYED EXPRESSION. To avoid any arguing over which driver took which horse the next day one stables run by a Mr Hobson allocated horses without any input from the drivers. This gives us the expression HOBSONS CHOICE. Incidentally, the many modern garages and repair shops for cabs are still gathered around Hackney.

Some of the laws created in those days, often for animal welfare, are still on the statute books. Odd as it may seem, a London taxi driver can still be arrested if he does not have A BALE OF HAY in his cab to feed his non-existent horse. In fact the strange space to the left of the cab driver that is often used for luggage (because the boot at the back of the cab is ludicrously small and really just for show) was originally designed for the hay! Taxi drivers are also legally still permitted to relieve themselves in public as long as they urinate up against their own rear axle (a provision originally introduced to enable squeaking rear wheels to be lubricated). It is not unknown to see a cabbie standing by the side of the road with both doors on that side open, providing a makeshift screen while he takes advantage of this law! Up until very recently cabs could not legally be hailed from the pavement, only at an official taxi point. The reason why cabs have such a good turning circle is that very early motorized cabs had no reverse gear – a bit like the horse-drawn carriages before them – and so they had to be able to turn around within a typical 25-foot-wide London road. They still have to.

10

Great British Pubs

Every pub name has its own fascinating history. Sometimes it was patriotism; sometimes political astuteness; and sometimes subtle rebellion. Celebrities and great military victories have also spawned their fair share of pub names and of course will continue to do so. Whatever the stories behind these welcome roadside signs, they are best discussed over a pint!

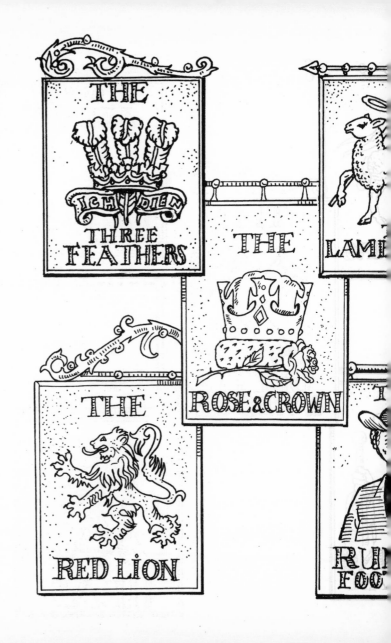

OLD ALBION

THE BEETLE & WEDGE

THE SARACEN'S HEAD

LAG

ING AN

Well, I never knew that . . .
. . . children were confused with elephants!

The signs hanging outside pubs and inns were originally painted so that illiterate commoners could identify a particular drinking establishment. Some medieval pubs and inns also served as a focal point for merchants and local moneylenders, and were even used for tax collection. These hostelries would often display a symbol outside to show prospective customers that they offered these services. This sign, based upon the cloth marked as a chequerboard that was used by the government to help record and calculate payments, has given its name to many pubs across the country: The Chequer Cloth or The Chequerboard, or simply THE CHEQUERS. Coincidentally, Lord Fitzwarren, who was responsible for licensing ale houses during the late 15th century, had a coat of arms which was a chequerboard. This too popularized the sign.

Infant is the Latin word for silent; hence the use of the word to describe a child so young that it cannot yet speak. *Infanta* was the title used by any child of a Spanish king who was not the first in line to the throne. This assumed that the heir to the throne should have more voice than his younger siblings and that therefore they should defer to his voice and be silent. Edward the First married one such Spanish daughter from Castile, who was known as the *'Infanta de Castile'*. This became a popular name for inns and pubs. Over time, though, the name was corrupted into similar-sounding English words, and so we get the pub name ELEPHANT AND CASTLE. Incidentally, the idea that some people are not worthy enough to be heard, and should therefore remain silent and simply do what they are told, was applied to the masses of medieval armies, who were usually peasants. Hence the word INFANTRY.

The late 14th-century coat of arms of Richard II was an albino male deer with a gold chain around its neck, better known as THE WHITE HART. This old name for a deer also gives the name of a village near an old royal deer park in Sussex, HARTFIELD. This is where the stories of *Winnie the*

Pooh are set, specifically the bridge – which is still there – where he used to throw sticks into a river with Christopher Robin and see whose stick travelled fastest. This game is now known throughout the world as POOH STICKS.

Well, I never knew that . . .
. . . the fiddling cat isn't musical at all

What was the animal heraldic symbol of Anne of Denmark, who became queen to James I at the beginning of the 17th century? The joke at the time was that it was a very cold version of the English regal animal, hence the colour – THE BLUE LION. When James I's very popular daughter married

Frederick, King of Bohemia, this prompted the appearance of an equally popular sign for new pubs, THE QUEEN OF BOHEMIA. Another popular choice was the breed of hunting dog used as a heraldic symbol of the Earl of Shrewsbury and also the family name: TALBOT.

Carpenters would often use a hammer-cum-mallet called a 'beetle' to drive in angled pieces of wood to strengthen constructions. From this we get the BEETLE AND WEDGE. The symbol of the Prince of Wales was established at the Battle of Crécy when Edward the Black Prince defeated the 14th-century King of Bohemia in personal combat and was awarded his heraldic symbol as a reward. This name became instantly popular with innkeepers throughout England: THE THREE FEATHERS.

When the Romans invaded Britain, the White Cliffs of Dover were the first part of coastline they saw. Using their word for white, *alba*, they called our island ALBION. Hence the pub name THE ALBION. Incidentally, other words from the same Latin root include the one for an animal with no pigmentation in its skin or fur: ALBINO, and the white part of an egg: ALBUMEN. Also, a blank book made up of unprinted white pages is an ALBUM.

The religious symbolism of Jesus Christ as the sacrificial lamb and a flag representing his bloody death through crucifixion became popular as crusaders returned from the Middle East in the form of the LAMB AND FLAG (of St George, the bloody cross). At the same time another sign became popular referring to one of the Arab invaders who had taken over Jerusalem and implying that the heathen had been decapitated by a brave crusader: THE SARACEN'S HEAD. A similar pub name with a similar grisly implication developed at the height of the Ottoman Empire (modern-day Turkey): THE TURK'S HEAD.

In the 14th century, when John of Gaunt was one of the most important figures in the country, many innkeepers named their inns after his heraldic symbol of the RED LION. However, it was not until James I of England (who was already James VI of Scotland) came to the throne in 1603 and specified that

he wanted to see the Scottish heraldic version of the Red Lion all over his newly United Kingdom that it became the most popular name for a pub in the country – which it still is today. However, many people did not like having a Scottish king, and certainly did not like having the Scottish symbol emblazoned all over England; and so there was another inn sign that became very popular with English nationalists wanting to link the traditional English emblem of the rose with the idea that the monarchy would be returned to English hands in the future. This is why we have so many pubs across the country that have strong associations as *English* pubs rather than *British* pubs, all named ROSE AND CROWN.

The name of the very large barrels used to transport wine and beer and, not surprisingly, the symbol of the Vintners' Company, have given us three very similar pub names: THE TUN, THE THREE TUNS and THE MASHED TUN. This is also why one measure of a ship's carrying capacity is called 'tunnage'. This measured in volume how many tuns (barrels) would fit into the hold, as opposed to 'tonnage' (with an 'o') which measures the carrying capacity in weight (tons). There is also another measure of the size of a ship, which is how many tons of water the ship displaces when it is afloat.

The heraldic emblem of the Earl of Oxford during the Wars of the Roses was a blue version of an existing coat of arms based upon a woodland animal that was very fierce if cornered, and one that people had to be very wary of annoying – a good message to convey to potential enemies: THE BLUE BOAR.

Yet another commonly found name is a corruption of the French phrase meaning 'faithful cat' – *la chatte fidèle* –

not, as many people think, a nursery rhyme: THE CAT AND FIDDLE.

A name derived from an inn that acted as a staging point where horses could be fed and watered or even changed, and where passengers could rest, was later adopted by smaller pubs that had no such traffic but wanted to capture the excitement and romance of long journeys: the COACH AND HORSES.

During the late medieval period a lot of meat, especially pork, was salted to preserve it. This made people thirsty, and given that water was often unsafe to drink everyone drank beer, although a less alcoholic version than we drink today. So some pubs were named after the food and a slang word for 'mouth': PIG AND WHISTLE. The idea that you cannot whistle with a dry mouth gave a very common usage of the word 'whistle' for mouth, especially related to drinking, as in the phrase for slaking your thirst, WET YOUR WHISTLE – which is why the word 'whistle' occurs in many old pub names.

An old village game involved securing a duck's wings to its sides and then releasing a dog to chase it into the village pond. As it could not fly away it would have to dive to escape the dog, creating much perverse excitement and fun – and the pub name THE DOG AND DUCK.

A brownish-reddish breed of cattle in the Middle Ages also gave rise to a pub name. Given that the majority of people worked on or near farms this was a good name to attract customers: THE RED COW. Another came from a popular medieval board game based upon farm geese being chased by a predator: FOX AND GEESE.

The heraldic symbol of Edward III, which supported his claim to the throne and suggested the dawning of a new age under his reign, led to many pubs being called THE RISING SUN.

Then there is a pub name which has two different derivations reflected in different pub signs. One source is early postal services. The second was the man who would clear people

away from in front of a nobleman's horse or carriage in a town, pay innkeepers and tolls, and help the coach out of mud or holes in the road. Pub signs showing the latter derivation usually depict him with a sturdy stick for this purpose: THE RUNNING FOOTMAN.

This next pub name is usually found in salubrious neighbourhoods of large towns or cities, or at least areas that used to be salubrious. It refers to the sedan chairs which were very popular before many streets were paved: THE TWO CHAIRMEN.

One story gives us two pub names. One refers to the flag of a saint, the other to the saint himself doing what he is most famous for doing. THE ST GEORGE often depicts a crusader or simply St George's flag; the alternative is the GEORGE AND DRAGON, where he is seen killing the dragon. Both became very popular when Richard the Lionheart adopted the flag of St George during the crusades. A similar sounding but unrelated pub sign usually refers to the King of England around the time of Napoleon, but sometimes is derived from his father, grandfather or son, all of whom had the same name: THE GEORGE.

Well, I never knew that . . .
. . . we remember Nelson's battle but forget Wellington's

Two British national heroes and *bêtes noires* of Napoleon also had many pubs named after them. The first to come to prominence died in 1805 at a sea battle which itself was also a popular name for pubs, TRAFALGAR. His flagship was even more popular as a pub name – THE VICTORY – and the man himself has given rise to three main pub names: THE NELSON, the LORD NELSON and THE ADMIRAL NELSON. Interestingly, the picture of Nelson is also the most popular picture for pubs called THE ADMIRAL. The second national hero had his greatest victory in Belgium in 1815, where his land forces famously beat Napoleon's army at Waterloo: THE DUKE OF WELLINGTON or just THE WELLINGTON. However, very few pubs are named after the battle itself.

11

Falconry –
The Sport of Kings

We may not understand how birds
of prey communicate, but we'd find
it hard to communicate ourselves
without the words and phrases
we've got from them.

Well, I never knew that . . .
. . . boozers get fed up and cadge a lift when they recover

When a hawk is ill it tends to drink more than usual. Medieval falconers noticed this and referred to such birds using a derivation of the French *boire* (to drink). This gives us a nickname for someone who drinks a lot of alcohol: BOOZER (from *vous bousez*). When the hunting birds had eaten enough food to satisfy their hunger they would lose interest in hunting and just want to sit on their perch, FED UP.

Hawks have very acute senses of hearing and sight and can become fidgety and uneasy if left to watch and listen to what was going on around them. Hence, to keep them quiet and peaceful they would often be hooded to prevent distractions:

OUT OF SIGHT, OUT OF MIND. If a bird did get fidgety it would tend to flap its wings and fly off, or even try to attack other birds. So it would be tied to its perch by a thin strip of leather, and be AT THE END OF ITS TETHER.

Hunting birds would often be kept in large cages which were then transported to a hunting area on a specially constructed tray. Combining the word 'cage' with the old word for 'carry', 'caddie', we get the name of these trays: cadges. The process of the birds being taken to the hunting area gives us the phrase to CADGE A LIFT. Now, these trays were unstable and the load of birds was difficult to carry, so that the men who did so would often walk awkwardly, as if they were old men. This led to the lords and ladies referring to these men as OLD CADGERS or OLD CODGERS.

These men who looked after the birds would sometimes bend the rules and take them to small groups of people to show them off, or allow visitors to take a close look at the birds, asking for a small payment in return. Hence TO CADGE SOME MONEY. This led to the word 'cadge' becoming associated with asking for favours and borrowing things that would never be returned – for example, CADGING A BEER from someone. The word 'codger' became associated with beggars and hence a phrase became common for someone who is old, dishevelled and reliant upon other people's generosity: AN OLD CODGER.

During the Middle Ages, many hawks were captured rather than bred. This meant that they had already had experience of hunting and capturing animals that would try to escape into a hedge. The older, more experienced hawks were named after the French word for hedge. Initially they would fight against the tethers and not eat properly and begin to look a little tussled and forlorn. Over time their name was used to describe beggars who had a similar look: HAGGARD, from the Old French word for 'hedge'. This developed into a word nowadays used exclusively for old and ugly women: HAG.

When a hunting bird has caught its prey and returned to its falconer it will typically retain a tight grip on its prey, and before long start to eat it. In order to get his hands on the prey the falconer would toss a small piece of raw meat to one side which the bird would then jump upon and eat, thus releasing its catch for the hunter. This was considered a good deal for both parties: A FAIR EXCHANGE IS NO ROBBERY. Falconry used to be a very status-driven sport, only the highest members of society being allowed to hunt with hawks. Buzzards, on the other hand, were considered to be of much lower status

and their use clearly defined one's lower social position. If someone's parentage, and therefore social status, was under question, they would said to be NEITHER HAWK NOR BUZZARD.

Fel was the Old French word for evil. Hence a heinous crime would be described as a *fel* crime or a FELONY. Over time the meaning in England evolved to mean a criminal who had committed an evil crime, and later any criminal: FELON. It also came to represent a sudden, wicked surprise attack, like a hawk swooping down upon an unsuspecting rabbit. For example, the enemy FELL on the camp at night. In falconry, a single attack or blow to kill the prey is described as ONE FELL SWOOP.

Thank you for reading this book. I do hope you said ...

Please read on and find out about:

- Locating your favourite phrases from the Index.
- How you can help make a brand new word.
- How to join WINKT the club.
- Other fascinating books in the series.
- 'Houston – we MAY have a problem'.
- How to discover your family's history, coat of arms and the origin of your surname.

Index

171

MESSAGE FROM THE AUTHOR

Please help create a brand new word!

'Well I Never Knew That!' – the story so far

Back in Victorian Dublin a man bet that he could get everyone in Dublin using a brand new word within 24 hours. He won the bet by having four letters scrawled all over the walls that night. The next morning everyone pointed at the letters, said them out loud and said, 'What is that?' The letters were Q U I Z. He had created the word QUIZ, which we now use to describe competitions where someone says – 'What is …?'

I foolishly made a similar bet in a pub – to create a brand new word and to get it into the dictionary. This turned into a gargantuan project of tracking down and linking the most intriguing, fascinating and funniest origins of everyday phrases and names in the English language. All the boring ones have been thrown away! That's how this series of books came about!

When friends read the first book they often said Well, I never knew that! – hence the name of the series. Then they shortened it to WINKT – the acronym of 'Well I Never Knew That!' meaning 'Wow!' or 'Gosh!' This is the new word: 'WINKT'!!!

'Please help finish the story!'

Now you've got WINKT the book – why not help create 'WINKT' the word and finish the story! All you have to do is send an email to word@winkt.com saying that 'I think "WINKT", meaning "Wow!" or "Gosh!" should be a new word in the dictionary.'

This will be added to the petition and when we get enough you will have played your part in creating a BRAND NEW WORD in the English language! In fact, if we get more than enough, we may even get into the *Guinness Book of World Records* as the most requested word ever! And, of course, tell your friends to email in as well. The more the merrier!

As a thank you I will give you free membership of WINKT the club!
Thank you,

Now you have enjoyed a WINKT book why not join WINKT the club?

As a member you can benefit from:

- Advanced information on new books before they are generally available.

- Information on other WINKT products, cards, posters, etc.

- Beautiful manuscript style scrolls that tell the professionally researched history and heritage of your family surname together with an historically accurate full colour coat of arms. Fascinating and eye catching presents either framed or unframed. We can also offer a scroll with two coat of arms – ideal for a wedding or anniversary present.

- The opportunity to get your name into the credits of a future WINKT book by offering a new WINKT expression.

- A newsletter with more fascinating derivations, members' questions, competitions and prizes.

- Occasional emails sent to you with fascinating new WINKT origins.

- Sets of approved WINKT questions for use in pub/trivia quizzes, parties or dinner parties.

- 'Ask Peter' service for the derivation of specific words or phrases.

- Join the campaign to get 'WINKT' recognised as an official word and enter the Guinness Book of World Records to get the most requested word ever!

And much, much more.

Simply register online at www.WINKT.com and get your friends and family to register too! Join the fun today!

Other books in the WINKT series due Autumn 2006

WHO PUT THE 'GREAT' IN GREAT BRITAIN?

THE HISTORY OF GREAT BRITAIN

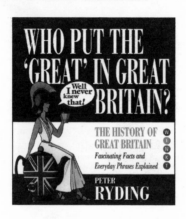

Do you know ...

... why England has three heraldic lions – because none of them were English!

... why Cromwell was such a 'whitewash', 'warts and all'?

... why we call our flag a 'Union JACK' – and why you may never have seen one?

... why a popular nursery rhyme teaches our children about destruction, boozing, pawning and child mortality? It's enough to make you 'pop your clogs'!

... and what is a 'cock-horse' anyway?

ISBN 0-9551525-3-4

DO SPIES WIN OLYMPIC MEDALS?

SPORTS, GAMES & GAMBLING

Do you know ...

... why going 'down like ninepins' may get you 'knocked into a cocked hat'?

... why we train Olympic athletes to be spies?

... why we call football 'soccer'?

... how you can play cards with Alexander the Great and Julius Caesar?

... why 'passing the buck' is not a 'good idea'?

ISBN 0-9551525-6-9

Other books in the WINKT series

DID ROMANS INVENT THE SPACE SHUTTLE?

THE ROMAN EMPIRE

Do you know ...

... how the Romans 'made a mint' when their city was destroyed?

... why they didn't just have vandals – they virtually invented them?

... how Roman sewers have helped specify modern trains and the Space Shuttle!

... why anyone paid a 'salary' owes it all to the Romans – especially if they are not 'worth their salt'?

... why the Romans gave us 'malaria'?

ISBN 0-9551525-5-0

NELSON AND THE ROYAL NAVY

Do you know ...

... why letting 'the cat out of the bag' may leave you a 'marked man'?

... why the 'Jack and Jill' nursery rhyme is really about sex?

... why you must 'pull your finger out' before 'firing a broadside' at someone?

... why it doesn't hurt the 'monkey' when its balls are frozen off?

... the connection between shopping malls and the Battle of Trafalgar?

ISBN 0-9551525-2-6
(2005 original edition ISBN 0-9551525-0-X)

Future WINKT books for release in 2007 and 2008

Log on to www.winkt.com to find out more.
Join the club and receive advanced information of new releases!

- Time, Astronomy and Astrology
- Food and Drink
- London and Londoners
- Knights and Warfare through the Ages
- Big Business and Great Brands

- Ancient Greece
- USA and The World
- Cockney Rhyming Slang
- and more!

You've read the book – now play the game!

WELL I NEVER KNEW THAT – THE ADVENTURE!

The fun and fast-moving interactive **DVD** and **TV GAME** with fascinating and intriguing pictures, photos and video clues.

10 games on a DVD disc – guaranteed no repeat questions.

The perfect gift for lovers of words, phrases, history and our national heritage.

Available from www.winkt.com Autumn 2006.

Also by the same author

'Houston – we MAY have a problem!'

How to spot business issues early and fix them.

ISBN 0-9551525-9-3

Copies can be ordered from www.peterryding.com

*'I commend this book to anyone who feels they MAY be facing business challenges …
amusing and entertaining but without pulling any punches.'*

SIR JOHN HARVEY-JONES MBE (of TV *Troubleshooter* fame)

*'This short book is the most straightforward and digestible piece of commercial
education that I have come across.'*

CHIEF EXECUTIVE OF THE SOCIETY OF TURNAROUND PROFESSIONALS

In the fast-paced business world of today everyone is under more stress than ever before. That includes CEOs and their directors. No wonder they need help. But how and when should they get that help?

This book provides the answer in a very short, illustrated and highly readable way. It is written by one of the UK's leading profit improvement experts and is specifically for CEOs and their leadership teams.

It tells the story of John, a CEO with a problem.

The trouble is, it has crept up on him and he doesn't know what to do.

'King Harold is too busy to see any salesmen right now.'

In fact, he doesn't really understand the severe implications for his business and for himself personally.

He then does the first of three critical things.

He gets help.

But is it too late?

If you haven't been there before, it is very tough to spot the problem, to identify which levers to pull, to know whom to believe and how to manage the various stakeholders around you. This book shows you what to do and what not to do.

'Reading this book could be the best spent thirty minutes of your career and save you a lot more than your job!'

SIR DIGBY JONES, DIRECTOR GENERAL OF THE CBI

To contact Peter please email peter@pathfinderpro.co.uk

Surname History and Coat of Arms

Do you know the origin of your surname?
Do you know the history of your family name from the middle ages?
Do you know the coat of arms or motto associated with it?
We do!

We specialise in providing professionally researched backgrounds to surnames and first names including coat of arms where relevant.

We can provide beautiful manuscript style scrolls either framed or unframed.

We can provide two coats of arms side by side for a special wedding or anniversary present.

We can even provide the history of a friend's or relative's first name and surname for a very personal and treasured historic gift.

Log on to www.WINKT.com and order yours now!